The Spokesman

War is Peace

Edited by Ken Coates

Published by Spokesman for the Bertrand Russell Peace Foundation

Spokesman 73 **2001**

CONTENTS

Cover photo: A B52 bombing Afghanistan.

Printed by the Russell Press Ltd., Nottingham, UK

ISSN 0262 7922

ISBN 0 85124 660 5

Subscriptions
Institutions £30.00
Individuals £20.00 (UK)
£25.00 (ex UK)

Back issues available on request

A CIP catalogue record for this book is available from the British Library

Published by the
Bertrand Russell Peace Foundation Ltd.,
Russell House
Bulwell Lane
Nottingham NG6 0BT
England
Tel. 0115 9784504
email:
elfeuro@compuserve.com
www.spokesmanbooks.com
www.russfound.org

Editorial

Power Play and the New World Chaos

Europe after the Second World War developed a strong culture of pacifism. Part of this was driven by internal motives. The movement towards European Union was undoubtedly stimulated by the felt need to eliminate tensions between France and Germany, and to make impossible new eruptions within the European continent. The establishment of the European Coal and Steel Community was, amongst other things, a deliberate attempt to fuse resources and overcome the national economic competition which could bring about a renewal of militarism.

Of course, all this unwound within the context of the Cold War, which, as it became more and more dependent on nuclear confrontation, aroused our own peace movements, for nuclear disarmament. Whilst not wishing to sentimentalise these different pacifisms[1], they undoubtedly became part of a wider culture[2], which was only partially eclipsed by the end of the Cold War, as a result of which we were proved wrong in our supposition that general nuclear disarmament might become an established fact.

Within the European pacific mindset was maintained a decades-long social consensus, the broadly social/Christian democrat commitment to full employment and welfare, now eroding under the influence of neo-liberalism.

The collapse of the Soviet Union gave an early impulse to a number of genuine European efforts to develop close co-operation in the renewal of Russia, and to move towards joint institutions which might guarantee the progress of disarmament. But in a relatively short time, the international stage was clearly taken over by the United States, which has followed a different policy, with considerable determination. Part of this has involved an exaggerated economic liberalism, which, although very one-sided, may not necessarily be belligerent. But another, nakedly militaristic, part of this doctrine was enunciated by Zbigniew Brzezinski (one-time National Security Adviser to President Carter), who formulated the doctrine that global domination follows the domination of Eurasia. This doctrine implied that the United States would follow a forward policy in respect of the former Soviet Union. So evolved the expansion of Nato, and the establishment of a new transitional organisation, the Partnership for Peace. This was seen as a kind of bridge to Nato for former neutrals, and above all for former members of the Warsaw Treaty and former republics of the Soviet Union itself. Peace movements, in their weakened state, paid some attention to the Eastward expansion of Nato, and often opposed the subversion of the neutrals, but they largely ignored the eastward progress of the Partnership for Peace which was able to mount joint Nato military exercises with the Ukraine, Georgia and some of the most important Central Asian Republics. All of these were not only directed against Russian military power, but threatened the erosion of Russian political influence. Unfortunately, the undermining of Russian power, in this case, implied the aggrandisement of the United States, which was already over-grand for its own mental health.

At the culmination of this process, the bombing of Yugoslavia caused great revulsion among the Russian political classes, so that the end of the Yeltsin regime brought Vladimir Putin into office, with an apparently more robust policy aimed at restoring Russian influence over the territories of the former Soviet Union. This was accompanied by an alarming new nuclear doctrine of 'first use' of nuclear weapons, as well as a ferocious intensification of repressive war in Chechnya.

Meantime, the American military were preparing the ground politically for the launch of a vast new technological offensive, with the comforting but misleading name of National Missile Defence. 'Son of Star Wars' as it has been more widely known, is a comprehensive plan for the militarisation of space, which implies the destruction not only of the Anti-Ballistic Missile Treaty, but also the Outer Space Treaty. The new surge of satellite weapons, and space-based lasers is all conceived within the overall doctrine of Full Spectrum Dominance, which is the official doctrine of the American military, and is nicely complementary with the Brzezinski schema.

The election of President Bush produced a number of unilateral initiatives which have alarmed the European partners of the United States, and aroused the great concern of public opinion around the world. In order to introduce his space-based military techniques, Bush made it plain that he was determined to repudiate the ABM Treaty, and demolish what he called 'the Cold War agreements' upon which contemporary arms control measures have all rested. At the same time, the United States unilaterally repudiated the result of the Kyoto negotiations on environmental protection, and undermined international agreements on landmines, small arms and biological weapons. The United States government also blocked moves to create an International Criminal Court, which may be seen as an ironical fact in the light of subsequent events.

By the summer of 2001, popular concern in Europe and the United States was already beginning to show itself in the growth of a number of peace movements.

The destruction of the World Trade Centre in New York, and the onslaught against the Pentagon in Washington, have changed international balances. The shock generated by these atrocities initially united world opinion in strong sympathy for their American victims. This sympathy remains strong. But when responses were considered, naturally most people thought in terms of the necessary actions of the United Nations and its relevant organs. Instead, a military response was developed, with the direct involvement of the United States and Britain, and with lesser and more indecisive involvement by certain selected Nato allies, and some other countries. Great efforts were made to involve Middle Eastern and Muslim States. But the initial alliance-building efforts produced uncertain results. Alienation and downright antipathy grew rapidly throughout the Arab world, and among Muslims from the Philippines and Indonesia across Pakistan to Saudi Arabia. A near revolutionary situation has been developing in Saudi Arabia, and it is reported that foreigners from the West dare not go out of doors. The American soldiers who are stationed in the country are confined to their base, and the Saudi royal family is deeply split on the question of how to get rid of them. Even the European allies have been showing increasing fractiousness, as the implications of the bombing of Afghanistan have become more apparent and more disturbing.

The original overtures to Russia and China were received with greater than normal diplomatic warmth, and in mid-October a wider 'coalition' announced itself with some official ceremony during the thirteenth Asia-Pacific Economic Co-operation ministerial meeting in Shanghai. This was attended by both Jiang Zemin and Vladimir Putin as well as George Bush. Yet within a very short time all these protestations of common cause began to look rickety. With the Middle East and the Muslim world in chaos, could the Brzezinski doctrine now be implemented in full force? With an Afghan war likely to spill over its frontiers into Pakistan on the one side, and former Soviet Central Asia on the other, the prospect could be one of very considerable tumult at the best, and quite possibly one of widespread war and destruction.

No doubt the awesome possibility of such a war has troubled the Russian Government, which has already suffered from the effects of destabilisation elsewhere. But Zbigniew Brzezinski, in outlining his proposals for the renewal of the great game in Central Asia, had opened the speculation that one variant of American policy in the region might involve the offer of a condominium to the Russian leaders, involving one or several special areas of joint action. Those leaders might be sceptical about such an offer, if they had read Brzezinski's blueprint:

> 'For the United States, Eurasian geostrategy involves the purposeful management of geostrategically dynamic states and the careful handling of geopolitically catalytic states, in keeping with the twin interests of America in the short-term preservation of its unique global power and in the long-run transformation of it into increasingly institutionalized global cooperation. To put it in a terminology that hearkens back to the more brutal age of ancient empires, the three grand imperatives of imperial geostrategy are to prevent collusion and maintain security dependence among the vassals, to keep tributaries pliant and protected, and to keep the barbarians from coming together.'[3]

Extrapolating from this theme, Brzezinski tells us that for the Americans,

> 'The most dangerous scenario would be a grand coalition of China, Russia, and perhaps Iran, an 'antihegemonic coalition united not by ideology but by complementary grievances.'[4]

Not surprisingly, Brzezinski thinks that preventing this may be a difficult task.

Hope springs eternal, and it is clear that the alliance builders who went to work after September 11th, wished to overcome this problem in one fell swoop, exploiting the grievances of all three countries against their adversaries in Afghanistan by including them in the Coalition against Terrorism. However, such an inclusive alliance was not to prove acceptable to the Iranians, and even the impressive results that had been obtained with the Russians and Chinese by the time of the Shanghai summit could be of rather short duration. But one thing is absolutely plain. Dominance, Full Spectrum or other, is absolutely incompatible with a democratically acceptable world order. To incorporate new subordinates under the prevailing domination will inhibit rather than encourage any development of democracy among them.

Whether we like it or not, this is bound to concern all the peace movements, and their concern will deepen, as the crisis extends itself.

Fortunately, it also concerns all those other movements which have already articulated their responses to global economic domination, debt, and the destruction of the natural environment. It is not difficult to see how the processes begun at Seattle and Porto Alegre, and continued in Genoa, share all the fundamental concerns of the new peace movement.

The immediate question for all of us is, how can we bring about a constructive convergence of these movements, which may well become the most important human resource, in the effort to save the world from new paroxysms of destruction?

Ken Coates

1 They were anything but rigorously consistent, especially in their attitudes to colonial wars.

2 As one prominent German pacifist puts it: 'You are certainly right about the motivation for the EU – sort of "taming" Germany and including it in a multinational regime. But another reason for this is also that all of Europe – and with aerospace included in the arsenal also for the island of Britain – has a century-old experience of "frontiers". "We" have friends and foes around us, border to border (particularly Germany from 1945 to 1990). For Europe with many nations so close to each other, and often hostile to each other, security for their own populations could only be achieved by co-operating with neigbouring countries, friends and foes. Europe has always lived in the knowledge of its vulnerability. This is a new experience for the United States. Also the horror of World War Two came only indirectly to the population of the United States, whereas most of Europe has a kind of collective memory of that time as a result of direct experience'.

3. Zbigniew Brzezinski, *The Grand Chessboard*, Basic Books, New York, p.40.

4. ibid p.55.

The algebra of infinite justice

Arundhati Roy

In the aftermath of the unconscionable 11th September suicide attacks on the Pentagon and the World Trade Centre, an American newscaster said: 'Good and Evil rarely manifest themselves as clearly as they did last Tuesday. People who we don't know, massacred people who we do. And they did so with contemptuous glee.'[1] Then he broke down and wept.

Here's the rub: America is at war against people it doesn't know (because they don't appear much on TV). Before it has properly identified or even begun to comprehend the nature of its enemy, the US Government has, in a rush of publicity and embarrassing rhetoric, cobbled together an 'International Coalition Against Terror', mobilized its army, its airforce, its navy and its media, and committed them to battle.

The trouble is that once America goes off to war, it can't very well return without having fought one. If it doesn't find its enemy, for the sake of the enraged folks back home, it will have to manufacture one. Once war begins, it will develop a momentum, a logic and a justification of its own, and we'll lose sight of why it's being fought in the first place.

What we're witnessing here is the spectacle of the world's most powerful country, reaching reflexively, angrily, for an old instinct to fight a new kind of war. Suddenly, when it comes to defending itself, America's streamlined warships, its cruise missiles and F-16 jets look like obsolete, lumbering things. As deterrence, its arsenal of nuclear bombs is no longer worth its weight in scrap. Box-cutters, penknives, and cold anger are the weapons with which the wars of the new century will be waged. Anger is the lock pick. It slips through customs unnoticed. Doesn't show up in baggage checks.

Who is America fighting? On the 20th of September, the FBI said that it had doubts about the identities of some of the hijackers. On the same day President George Bush said he knew exactly who the terrorists were and which

Arundhati Roy, the Booker Prize-winning author of The God *of* Small Things, *is a foremost campaigner against the war on Afghanistan. This article is dated 24th September 2001, and was sent from New Delhi.*

governments were supporting them.[2] It sounds as though the President knows something that the FBI and the American public don't.

In his 20th September address to the US Congress, President George Bush called the enemies of America 'Enemies of Freedom'. 'Americans are asking why do they hate us?' he said. 'They hate our freedoms – our freedom of religion, our freedom of speech, our freedom to vote and assemble and disagree with each other'.[3] People are being asked to make two leaps of faith here. First, to assume that The Enemy is who the US government says it is, even though it has no substantial evidence to support that claim. And second, to assume that The Enemy's motives are what the US government says they are, and there's nothing to support that either.

For strategic, military and economic reasons, it is vital for the US government to persuade the American public that America's commitment to freedom and democracy and the American Way of Life is under attack. In the current atmosphere of grief, outrage and anger, it's an easy notion to peddle. However, if that were true, it's reasonable to wonder why the symbols of America's economic and military dominance – the World Trade Centre and the Pentagon – were chosen as the targets of the attacks. Why not the Statue of Liberty? Could it be that the stygian anger that led to the attacks has its taproot not in American freedom and democracy, but in the US Government's record of commitment and support to exactly the opposite things – to military and economic terrorism, insurgency, military dictatorship, religious bigotry and unimaginable genocide (outside America)?

It must be hard for ordinary Americans so recently bereaved, to look up at the world with their eyes full of tears and encounter what might appear to them to be indifference. It isn't indifference. It's just augury. An absence of surprise. The tired wisdom of knowing that what goes around, eventually comes around. American people ought to know that it is not them, but their government's policies that are so hated. All of us have been moved by the courage and grace shown by America's firefighters, rescue workers and ordinary office goers in the days that followed the attacks. American people can't possibly doubt that they themselves, their extraordinary musicians, their writers, their actors, their spectacular sportsmen and their cinema, are universally welcomed.

America's grief at what happened has been immense and immensely public. It would be grotesque to expect it to calibrate or modulate its anguish. However, it will be a pity if, instead of using this as an opportunity to try and understand why September 11th happened, Americans use it as an opportunity to usurp the whole world's sorrow to mourn and avenge only their own. Because then it falls to the rest of us to ask the hard questions and say the harsh things. And for our pains, for our bad timing, we will be disliked, ignored and perhaps eventually silenced.

The world will probably never know what motivated those particular hijackers who flew planes into those particular American buildings. They were not glory boys. They left no suicide notes, no political messages, no organization has claimed credit for the attacks. All we know is that their belief in what they were doing outstripped the natural human instinct for survival or any desire to be remembered. It's almost as though they could not scale down the enormity of their rage to anything smaller than their deeds. And what they did has blown a hole in the world as we knew it. In the absence of information, politicians, political commentators and writers (like myself) will invest the act with their own politics, with their own interpretations. This speculation, this analysis of the political climate in which the attacks took place, can only be a good thing.

But war is looming large. Whatever remains to be said, must be said quickly.

Before America places itself at the helm of the 'international coalition against terror', before it invites (and coerces) countries to actively participate in its almost godlike mission – called Operation Infinite Justice until it was pointed out that this could be seen as an insult to Muslims, who believe that only Allah can mete out infinite justice, and was renamed Operation Enduring Freedom – it would help if some small clarifications are made. For example, Infinite Justice/Enduring Freedom for whom? Is this America's War Against Terror in America or against Terror in general? What exactly is being avenged here? Is it the tragic loss of almost 7000 lives, the gutting of 15 million square feet of office space in Manhattan[4], the destruction of a section of the Pentagon, the loss of several hundreds of thousands of jobs, the potential bankruptcy of some airline companies and the crash of the New York Stock Exchange? Or is it more than that?

In 1996, Madeleine Albright, then the US Ambassador to the United Nations, was asked on national television what she felt about the fact that 500,000 Iraqi children had died as a result of US economic sanctions. She replied that it was 'a very hard choice,' but that all things considered, 'we think the price is worth it.'[5] Albright never lost her job for saying this. She continued to travel the world representing the views and aspirations of the US Government. More pertinently, the sanctions against Iraq remain in place. Children continue to die.

So here we have it. The equivocating distinction between civilization and savagery, between the 'massacre of innocent people' or, if you like, 'a clash of civilizations' and 'collateral damage'. The sophistry and fastidious algebra of Infinite Justice. How many dead Iraqis will it take to make the world a better place? How many dead Afghans for every dead American? How many dead children for every dead man? How many dead mujahideen for each dead investment banker?

As we watch mesmerized, Operation Enduring Freedom unfolds on TV monitors across the world. A coalition of the world's superpowers is closing in on Afghanistan, one of the poorest, most ravaged, war-torn countries in the world, whose ruling Taliban government is sheltering Osama Bin Laden, the man being held responsible for the September 11th attacks. The only thing in Afghanistan that could possibly count as collateral value is its citizenry. (Among them, half a million maimed orphans. There are accounts of hobbling stampedes that occur when artificial limbs are airdropped into remote, inaccessible villages.)[6] Afghanistan's economy is in a shambles. In fact, the problem for an invading army is that Afghanistan has no conventional co-ordinates or sign-posts to plot on a map – no military bases, no industrial complexes, no water treatment plants. Farms have been turned into mass graves. The countryside is littered with land mines – ten million is the most recent estimate.[7] The American army would first have to clear the mines and build roads in order to take its soldiers in. Fearing an attack from America, one million citizens have fled from their homes and arrived at the border between Pakistan and Afghanistan. The UN estimates that there are 8 million Afghan citizens who will need emergency aid.[8] As supplies run out – Food and Aid agencies have been evacuated – the BBC reports that one of the worst humanitarian disasters of recent times has begun to unfold.[9] Witness the Infinite Justice of the new century. Civilians starving to death, while they're waiting to be killed.

In America there has been rough talk of 'bombing Afghanistan back to the stone-age'. Someone please break the news that Afghanistan is already there.[10] And if it's any consolation, America played no small part in helping it on its way. The American people may be a little fuzzy about where exactly Afghanistan is (we hear reports that there's a run on maps of the country), but the US Government and Afghanistan are old friends.[11] In 1979, after the Soviet invasion of Afghanistan, the CIA and Pakistan's ISI (Inter Services Intelligence) launched the CIA's largest covert operation since the Vietnam war.[12] Their purpose was to harness the energy of Afghan resistance to the Soviets and expand it into a holy war, an Islamic jihad, which would turn Muslim countries within the Soviet Union against the Communist regime and eventually de-stabilize it. When it began, it was meant to be the Soviet Union's Vietnam. It turned out to be much more than that. Over the years, through the ISI, the CIA funded and recruited tens of thousands of radical mujahideen from 40 Islamic countries as soldiers for America's proxy war.[13] The rank and file of the mujahideen were unaware that their jihad was actually being fought on behalf of Uncle Sam. (The irony is that America was equally unaware that it was financing a future war against itself).

In 1989, after being bloodied by ten years of relentless conflict, the Russians withdrew, leaving behind a civilization reduced to rubble. Civil war in Afghanistan raged on. The jihad spread to Chechnya, Kosovo and eventually to Kashmir. The CIA continued to pour in money and military equipment, but the overheads had become immense, and more money was needed. The mujahideen ordered farmers to plant opium as a 'revolutionary tax'.[14] Under the protection of the ISI hundreds of heroin processing laboratories were set up across Afghanistan. Within two years of the CIA's arrival, the Pakistan-Afghanistan borderland had become the biggest producer of heroin in the world, and the single biggest source on American streets. The annual profits, said to be between 100 and 200 billion dollars, were ploughed back into training and arming militants.[15]

In 1996, the Taliban – then a marginal sect of dangerous, hard-line fundamentalists – fought its way to power in Afghanistan. It was funded by the ISI, that old cohort of the CIA, and supported by many political parties in

Pakistan.[16] The Taliban unleashed a regime of terror. Its first victims were its own people, particularly women. It closed down girls' schools, dismissed women from government jobs, enforced Sharia laws under which women deemed to be 'immoral' are stoned to death, and widows guilty of being adulterous are buried alive.[17] Given the Taliban government's human rights track record, it seems unlikely that it will in any way be intimidated or swerved from its purpose by the prospect of war, or the threat to the lives of its civilians.

After all that has happened, can there be anything more ironic than Russia and America joining hands to re-destroy Afghanistan? The question is, can you destroy destruction? Dropping more bombs on Afghanistan will only shuffle the rubble, scramble some old graves and disturb the dead. The desolate landscape of Afghanistan was the burial ground of Soviet Communism and the springboard of a uni-polar world dominated by America. It made the space for neo-capitalism and corporate globalization, again dominated by America. And now Afghanistan is poised to become the graveyard for the unlikely soldiers who fought and won this war for America.

And what of America's trusted ally? Pakistan too has suffered enormously. The US Government has not been shy of supporting military dictators who have blocked the idea of democracy from taking root in the country. Before the CIA arrived, there was a small rural market for opium in Pakistan. Between 1979 and 1985, the number of heroin addicts grew from next to nothing to a massive number.[18] Even before September 11th there were millions of Afghan refugees living in tented camps along the border. Pakistan's economy is crumbling. Sectarian violence, globalization's Structural Adjustment programmes and drug lords are tearing the country to pieces.[19] Set up to fight the Soviets, the terrorist training centres and madrassas, sown like dragon's teeth across the country, produced fundamentalists with tremendous popular appeal within Pakistan itself. The Taliban, which the Pakistan Government has supported, funded and propped up for years, has material and strategic alliances with Pakistan's own political parties.[20] Now the US government is asking (asking?) Pakistan to garrot the pet it has hand-reared in its backyard for so many years. President Musharraf, having pledged his support to the US, could well find he has something resembling civil war on his hands.[21]

India, thanks in part to its geography, and in part to the vision of its former leaders, has so far been fortunate enough to be left out of this Great Game. Had it been drawn in, it's more than likely that our democracy, such as it is, would not have survived. Today, as some of us watch in horror, the Indian Government is furiously gyrating its hips, begging the US to set up its base in India rather than Pakistan.[22] Having had this ringside view of Pakistan's sordid fate, it isn't just odd, it's unthinkable, that India should want to do this. Any Third World country with a fragile economy and a complex social base, should know by now that to invite a Superpower such as America in, (whether it says it's staying or just passing through), would be like inviting a brick to drop through your winsdscreen.

In the media blitz that followed the September 11th, mainstream TV stations largely ignored the story of America's involvement with Afghanistan. So, to those unfamiliar with the story, the coverage of the attacks could have been moving, disturbing and perhaps to cynics, self-indulgent. However, to those of us who are familiar with Afghanistan's recent history, American television coverage and the rhetoric of the 'International Coalition Against Terror' is just plain insulting. America's 'free press' like its 'free market' has a lot to account for.

Operation Enduring Freedom is ostensibly being fought to uphold the American Way of Life. It'll probably end up undermining it completely. It will spawn more anger and more terror across the world. For ordinary people in America, it will mean lives lived in a climate of sickening uncertainty: will my child be safe in school? Will there be nerve gas in the subway? A bomb in the cinema hall? Will my love come home tonight? There have been warnings about the possibility of biological warfare – small pox, bubonic plague, anthrax – the deadly payload of innocuous crop duster aircraft.[23] Being picked off a few at a time may end up being worse than being annihilated all at once by a nuclear bomb.

The US Government, and no doubt governments all over the world, will use the climate of war as an excuse to curtail civil liberties, deny free speech, lay off workers, harass ethnic and religious minorities, cut back on public spending and divert huge amounts of money to the defence industry. To what purpose? President George Bush can no more 'rid the world of evildoers' than he can stock it with saints.[24] It's absurd for the US Government to even toy with the notion that it can stamp out terrorism with more violence and oppression. Terrorism is the symptom, not the disease. Terrorism has no country. It's transnational, as global an enterprise as Coke or Pepsi or Nike. At the first sign of trouble, terrorists can pull up stakes and move their 'factories' from country to country in search of a better deal. Just like the multi-nationals.

Terrorism as a phenomenon may never go away. But if it is to be contained, the first step is for America to at least acknowledge that it shares the planet with other nations, with other human beings, who, even if they are not on TV, have loves and griefs and stories and songs and sorrows and, for heaven's sake, rights. Instead, when Donald Rumsfeld, the US Defence Secretary, was asked what he would call a victory in America's New War, he said that if he could convince the world that Americans must be allowed to continue with their way of life, he would consider it a victory.[25]

The 11th September attacks were a monstrous calling card from a world gone horribly wrong. The message may have been written by Bin Laden (who knows?) and delivered by his couriers, but it could well have been signed by the ghosts of the victims of America's old wars.

The millions killed in Korea, Vietnam and Cambodia, the 17,500 killed when Israel – backed by the US – invaded Lebanon in 1982, the tens of thousands of Iraqis killed in Operation Desert Storm, the thousands of Palestinians who have died fighting Israel's occupation of the West Bank.[26] And the millions who died, in Yugoslavia, Somalia, Haiti, Chile, Nicaragua, El Salvador, the Dominican Republic, Panama, at the hands of all the terrorists, dictators and genocidists who the American Government supported trained, bankrolled and supplied with arms. And this is far from being a comprehensive list.

For a country involved in so much warfare and conflict, the American people have been extremely fortunate. The strikes on September 11th were only the second on American soil in over a century. The first was Pearl Harbor. The reprisal for this took a long route, but ended with Hiroshima and Nagasaki. This time the world waits with bated breath for the horrors to come.

Someone recently said that if Osama Bin Laden didn't exist, America would have had to invent him.[27] But in a way, America did invent him. He was among the jihadis who moved to Afghanistan in 1979 when the CIA commenced its operations there. Bin Laden has the distinction of being created by the CIA and wanted by the FBI. In the course of a fortnight he has been promoted from Suspect, to Prime Suspect, and then, despite the lack of any real evidence, straight up the charts to being 'wanted dead or alive'.

From all accounts, it will be impossible to produce evidence (of the sort that would stand scrutiny in a court of law) to link Bin Laden to the September 11th attacks.[28] So far, it appears that the most incriminating piece of evidence against him is the fact that he has not condemned them. From what is known about the location of Bin Laden and the living conditions from which he operates, it's entirely possible that he did not personally plan and carry out the attacks – that he is the inspirational figure, 'the CEO of the Holding Company'.[29] The Taliban's response to US demands for the extradition of Bin Laden has been uncharacteristically reasonable: Produce the evidence, then we'll hand him over. President Bush's response is that the demand is 'non-negotiable'.[30]

(While talks are on for the extradition of CEOs – can India put in a side-request for the extradition of Warren Anderson of the USA? He was the Chairman of Union Carbide, responsible for the 1984 Bhopal gas leak that killed 16,000 people. We have collated the necessary evidence. It's all in the files. Could we have him, please?)[31]

But who is Osama Bin Laden really?

Let me rephrase that. What is Osama Bin Laden?

He's America's family secret. He is the American President's dark *doppelgänger*. The savage twin of all that purports to be beautiful and civilized. He has been sculpted from the spare rib of a world laid to waste by America's foreign policy: its gunboat diplomacy, its nuclear arsenal, its vulgarly stated policy of 'full spectrum dominance', its chilling disregard for non-American lives, its barbarous military interventions, its support for despotic and dictatorial regimes, its merciless economic agenda that has munched through the economies of poor countries like a cloud of locusts.[32] Its marauding multi-nationals who are taking over the air we breathe, the ground we stand on, the water we drink, the thoughts we think.

Now that the family secret has been spilled, the twins are blurring into one another and gradually becoming interchangeable. Their guns, bombs, money and drugs have been going around in the loop for a while. (The Stinger missiles that will greet US helicopters were supplied by the CIA. The heroin used by America's drug-addicts comes from Afghanistan. The Bush Administration recently gave Afghanistan a $43 million subsidy for a 'war on drugs'...)[33] Now they've even begun to borrow each other's rhetoric. Each refers to the other as 'the head of the snake'. Both invoke God and use the loose millenarian currency of Good and Evil as their terms of reference. Both are engaged in unequivocal political crimes. Both are dangerously armed – one with the nuclear arsenal of the obscenely powerful, the other with the incandescent, destructive power of the utterly hopeless. The fireball and the ice pick. The bludgeon and the axe. The important thing to keep in mind is that neither is an acceptable alternative to the other.

President Bush's ultimatum to the people of the world – 'Either you are with us or you are with the terrorists' – is a piece of presumptuous arrogance.[34]

It's not a choice that people want to, need to, or should have to make.

References

1. Fox News, September 17, 2001.
2. Marc Levine, 'New Suspect Arrested, But Doubts Grow Over Terrorists' Identities,' Agence France-Presse, September 21, 2001.
3. President George W. Bush, Address to Joint Session of Congress, 'The September 11th, 2001, Terrorist Attacks on the United States,' Federal News Service, September 20, 2001.
4. See Elsa Brenner, 'Hoping to Fill the Need for Office Space,' *New York Times* (Westchester Weekly Edition), September 23, 2001, p. 3.
5. Leslie Stahl, 'Punishing Saddam,' produced by Catherine Olian, CBS, *60 Minutes,* May 12, 1996.
6. See Tamim Ansary, 'Bomb Afghanistan Back to Stone Age? It's Been Done,' *Providence Journal,* September 22, 2001, p. B7.
7. Thomas E. Ricks, 'Land Mines, Aging Missiles Pose Threat,' *Washington Post,* September 25, 2001, p. A15. See also Danna Harman, 'Digging up Angola's Deadly Litter,' *Christian Science Monitor,* July 27, 2001, p. 6.
8. See Barry Bearak, 'Misery Hangs Over Afghanistan After Years of War and Drought,' *New York Times,* September 24, 2001, p. B3; Rajiv Chandrasekaran and Pamela Constable, 'Panicked Afghans Flee to Border Area,' *Washington Post,* September 23, 2001, p. A30; Catherine Solyom, 'Exhibit a Glimpse Into Refugee Life,' *The Gazette* (Montreal), September 21, 2001, p. A13; and Raymond Whitaker, Agence France-Presse, 'Pakistan Fears for Seven Million Refugees as Winter Looms,' *The Independent* (London), September 27, 2001, p. 4.
9. BBC, 'Aid Shortage Adds to Afghan Woes,' September 22, 2001. Available online at http://news.bbc.co.uk/hi/english/world/south_asia/newsid_1556000/1556117.stm.

10. See Tamim Ansary, 'Bomb Afghanistan Back to Stone Age? It's Been Done,' *Providence Journal,* September 22, 2001, p. B7.
11. See Paul Leavitt, 'Maps of Afghanistan Now in Short Supply,' *USA Today,* September 18, 2001, p. 13A.
12. *Washington* Post, February 7, 1985, quoted in Raja Anwar, *The Tragedy of Afghanistan: A First-Hand Account,* trans. Khalid Hasan (New York and London: Verso, 1988), p. 232; 'Inside the Taliban: U.S. Helped Cultivate the Repressive Regime Sheltering bin Laden,' *Seattle Times,* September 19, 2001, p. A3; and Andrew Duffy, 'Geographic Warriors,' *Ottawa Citizen,* September 23, 2001, p. C4.
13. On the CIA connection, see Steve Coll, 'Anatomy of a Victory: CIA's Covert Afghan War,' *Washington Post,* July 19, 1992, p. A1; Steve Coll, 'In CIA's Covert Afghan War, Where to Draw the Line Was Key,' *Washington Post,* July 20, 1992, p. A1; Tim Weiner, 'Blowback From the Afghan Battlefield,' *New York Times Magazine,* March 13, 1994, p. 6: 53; and Ahmed Rashid, 'The Making of a Terrorist,' *Straits Times* (Singapore), September 23, 2001, p. 26.
14. See Scott Baldauf, 'Afghans Try Opium-Free Economy,' *Christian Science Monitor,* April 3, 2001, p. 1.
15. See David Kline, 'Asia's "Golden Crescent" Heroin Floods the West,' *Christian Science Monitor,* November 9, 1982, p. 1; David Kline, 'Heroin's Trail from Poppy Fields to the West,' *Christian Science Monitor,* November 10, 1982, p. 1; and Rahul Bedi, 'The Assassins and Drug Dealers Now Helping US Intelligence,' *Daily Telegraph* (London), September 26, 2001, p. 10.
16. See Peter Popham, 'Taliban Monster That Was Launched by the US,' *The Independent* (London), September 17, 2001, p. 4.
17. See Suzanne Goldenberg, 'Mullah Keeps Taliban on a Narrow Path,' *Guardian* (London), August 17, 1998, p. 12.
18. See David K. Willis, 'Pakistan Seeks Help from Abroad to Stem Heroin Flow,' *Christian Science Monitor,* February 28, 1984, p. 11.
19. See Farhan Bokhari, 'Pakistan: Living in Shadow of Debt Mountain,' *Financial Times* (London), March 6, 2001, Survey: Pakistan, p. 4.
20. See Douglas Frantz, 'Sentiment in Pakistani Town Is Ardently Pro-Taliban,' *New York Times,* September 27, 2001, p. B1; Rahul Bedi, 'The Assassins and Drug Dealers Now Helping US Intelligence,' *Daily Telegraph* (London), September 26, 2001, p. 10.
21. See Edward Luce, 'Pakistan Nervousness Grows as Action Nears,' *Financial Times* (London), September 27, 2001, p. 6.
22. See Angus Donald and Khozem Merchant, 'Concern at India's Support for US,' *Financial Times* (London), September 21, 2001, p. 14.
23. See Jeff Greenfield and David Ensor, 'America's New War: Weapons of Terror,' CNN, *Greenfield at Large,* September 24, 2001.
24. Jim Drinkard, 'Bush Vows to "Rid the World of Evildoers,"' *USA Today,* September 17, 2001, p. 1A.
25. Secretary of Defense Donald Rumsfeld, Special Defense Briefing, 'Developments Concerning Attacks on the Pentagon and the World Trade Center Last Week,' Federal News Service, September 20, 2001.
26. See Robert Fisk, 'This Is Not a War on Terror, It's a Fight Against America's Enemies,' *The Independent* (London), September 25, 2001, p. 4.
27. George Monbiot, 'The Need for Dissent,' *Guardian* (London), September 18, 2001, p. 17.

28. See Michael Slackman, 'Terrorism Case Illustrates Difficulty of Drawing Tangible Ties to Al Qaeda,' *Los Angeles Times,* September 22, 2001, p. A1.
29. See Tim Russert, 'Secretary of State Colin Powell Discusses America's Preparedness for the War on Terrorism,' NBC, *Meet the Press,* September 23, 2001.
30. See T. Christian Miller, 'A Growing Global Chorus Calls for Proof,' *Los Angeles Times,* September 24, 2001, p. A10, and Dan Rather, 'President Bush's Address to Congress and the Nation,' CBS, *CBS News Special Report,* September 20, 2001.
31. See Nityanand Jayaraman and Peter Popham, 'Work Halts at Indian Unilever Factory After Poisoning Alert,' *The Independent* (London), March 11th, 2001, p. 19.
32. See Jack Hitt, 'Battlefield: Space,' *New York Times Magazine,* August 5, 2001, p. 6: 30.
33. See Colin Nickerson and Indira A.R. Lakshmanan, 'America Prepares the Global Dimension,' *Boston Globe,* September 27, 2001, p. A1; Barbara Crossette, 'Taliban's Ban On Poppy A Success, U.S. Aides Say,' *New York Times,* May 20, 2001, p. 1: 7; and Christopher Hitchens, 'Against Rationalization,' *The Nation* 273: 10 (October 8, 2001), p. 8.
34. President George W. Bush, Address to Joint Session of Congress, 'The September 11th, 2001, Terrorist Attacks on the United States,' Federal News Service, September 20, 2001.

War is Peace

Arundhati Roy

This second article about the war on Afghanistan is dated 16th October 2001.

As darkness deepened over Afghanistan on Sunday 7th October 2001, the US government, backed by the International Coalition Against Terror (the new, amenable surrogate for the United Nations), launched air strikes against Afghanistan. TV channels lingered on computer-animated images of cruise missiles, stealth bombers, tomahawks, 'bunker-busting' missiles and Mark 82 high drag bombs. All over the world, little boys watched goggle-eyed and stopped clamouring for new video games.

The UN, reduced now to an ineffective acronym, wasn't even asked to mandate the air strikes. (As Madeleine Albright once said, 'We will behave multilaterally when we can, and unilaterally when we must.') The 'evidence' against the terrorists was shared amongst friends in the 'Coalition'. After conferring, they announced that it didn't matter whether or not the 'evidence' would stand up in a court of law. Thus, in an instant, were centuries of jurisprudence carelessly trashed.

Nothing can excuse or justify an act of terrorism, whether it is committed by religious fundamentalists, private militia, people's resistance movements – or whether it's dressed up as a war of retribution by a recognised government. The bombing of Afghanistan is not revenge for New York and Washington. It is yet another act of terror against the people of the world. Each innocent person that is killed must be added to, not set off against, the grisly toll of civilians who died in New York and Washington.

People rarely win wars, governments rarely lose them. People get killed. Governments moult and regroup, hydra-headed. They use flags first to shrink-wrap peoples' minds and smother thought, and then as ceremonial shrouds to bury their willing dead. On both sides, in Afghanistan as well as America, civilians are now hostage to the actions of their own governments. Unknowingly, ordinary people in both countries share a common bond

– they have to live with the phenomenon of blind, unpredictable terror. Each batch of bombs that is dropped on Afghanistan is matched by a corresponding escalation of mass hysteria in America about anthrax, more hijackings and other terrorist acts.

There is no easy way out of the spiralling morass of terror and brutality that confronts the world today. It is time now for the human race to hold still, to delve into its wells of collective wisdom, both ancient and modern. What happened on September 11th changed the world forever. Freedom, progress, wealth, technology, war – these words have taken on new meaning. Governments have to acknowledge this transformation, and approach their new tasks with a modicum of honesty and humility. Unfortunately, up to now, there has been no sign of any introspection from the leaders of the International Coalition. Or the Taliban.

When he announced the air strikes, President George Bush said, 'We're a peaceful nation.' America's favourite Ambassador, Tony Blair, (who also holds the portfolio of Prime Minister of the UK), echoed him: 'We're a peaceful people.'

So now we know. Pigs are horses. Girls are boys. War is Peace.

Speaking at the FBI headquarters a few days later, President Bush said,

'This is our calling. This is the calling of the United States of America. The most free nation in the world. A nation built on fundamental values that reject hate, reject violence, rejects murderers and rejects evil. We will not tire.'

Here is a list of the countries that America has been at war with – and bombed – since World War Two: China (1945-46, 1950-53), Korea (1950-53), Guatemala (1954, 1967-69), Indonesia (1958), Cuba (1959-60), the Belgian Congo (1964), Peru (1965), Laos (1964-73), Vietnam (1961-73), Cambodia (1969-70), Grenada (1983), Libya (1986), El Salvador (1980s), Nicaragua (1980s), Panama (1989), Iraq (1991-99), Bosnia (1995), Sudan (1998), Yugoslavia (1999). And now Afghanistan.

Certainly it does not tire – this, the Most Free nation in the world. What freedoms does it uphold? Within its borders, the freedoms of speech, religion, thought; of artistic expression, food habits, sexual preferences (well, to some extent) and many other exemplary, wonderful things. Outside its borders, the freedom to dominate, humiliate and subjugate usually in the service of America's real religion, the 'free market'. So when the US government christens a war 'Operation Infinite Justice', or 'Operation Enduring Freedom', we in the Third World feel more than a tremor of fear. Because we know that Infinite Justice for some means Infinite Injustice for others. And Enduring Freedom for some means Enduring Subjugation for others.

The International Coalition Against Terror is largely a cabal of the richest countries in the world. Between them, they manufacture and sell almost all of the world's weapons, they possess the largest stockpile of weapons of mass destruction – chemical, biological and nuclear. They have fought the most wars, account for most of the genocide, subjection, ethnic cleansing and human rights violations in modern history, and have sponsored, armed and financed untold numbers of dictators and despots. Between them, they have worshipped, almost deified, the cult of violence and war. For all its appalling sins, the Taliban just isn’t in the same league.

The Taliban was compounded in the crumbling crucible of rubble, heroin and landmines in the backwash of the Cold War. Its oldest leaders are in their early forties. Many of them are disfigured and handicapped, missing an eye, an arm or a leg. They grew up in a society scarred and devastated by war. Between the Soviet Union and America, over 20 years, about $45 billion worth of arms and ammunition was poured into Afghanistan. The latest weaponry was the only shard of modernity to intrude upon a thoroughly medieval society. Young boys – many of them orphans – who grew up in those times, had guns for toys, never knew the security and comfort of family life, never experienced the company of women. Now, as adults and rulers, the Taliban beat, stone, rape and brutalize women, they don't seem to know what else to do with them. Years of war has stripped them of gentleness, inured them to kindness and human compassion. Now they’ve turned their monstrosity on their own people. They dance to the percussive rhythms of bombs raining down around them.

With all due respect to President Bush, the people of the world do not have to choose between the Taliban and the US Government. All the beauty of human civilization – our art, our music, our literature – lies beyond these two fundamentalist, ideological poles. There is as little chance that the people of the world can all become middle-class consumers as there is that they will all embrace any one particular religion. The issue is not about Good versus Evil or Islam versus Christianity as much as it is about space. About how to accommodate diversity, how to contain the impulse towards hegemony, every kind of hegemony, economic, military, linguistic, religious and cultural. Any ecologist will tell you how dangerous and fragile a monoculture is. A hegemonic world is like having a government without a healthy opposition. It becomes a kind of dictatorship. It's like putting a plastic bag over the world, and preventing it from breathing. Eventually, it will be torn open.

One and a half million Afghan people lost their lives in the 20 years of conflict that preceded this new war. Afghanistan was reduced to rubble, and now, the rubble is being pounded into finer dust. By the second day of the air strikes, US pilots were returning to their bases without dropping their assigned payload of bombs. As one pilot put it, Afghanistan is ‘not a target-rich environment’. At a press briefing at the Pentagon, Donald Rumsfeld, US Defence Secretary, was asked if America had run out of targets. ‘First we’re going to re-hit targets,’ he said, ‘and second, we're not running out of targets, Afghanistan is...’ This was greeted with gales of laughter in the Briefing Room.

By the third day of the strikes, the US Defence Department boasted that it had ‘achieved air supremacy over Afghanistan’ (Did they mean that they had destroyed both, or maybe all sixteen, of Afghanistan’s planes?)

On the ground in Afghanistan, the Northern Alliance – the Taliban’s old enemy, and therefore the International Coalition's newest friend – is making headway in its push to capture Kabul. (For the archives, let it be said that the Northern Alliance's track record is not very different from the Taliban's. But for now, because it's inconvenient, that little detail is being glossed over.) The visible, moderate, 'acceptable' leader of the Alliance, Ahmed Shah Masud, was killed in a suicide-bomb attack early in September. The rest of the Northern Alliance is a brittle confederation of brutal warlords, ex-communists and unbending clerics. It is a disparate group divided along ethnic lines, some of whom have tasted power in Afghanistan in the past.

Until the US air strikes, the Northern Alliance controlled about 5% of the geographical area of Afghanistan. Now, with the Coalition's help and 'air cover', it is poised to topple the Taliban. Meanwhile, Taliban soldiers, sensing imminent defeat, have begun to defect to the Alliance. So the fighting forces are busy switching sides and changing uniforms. But in an enterprise as cynical as this one, it seems to matter hardly at all. Love is hate, north is south, peace is war.

Among the global powers, there is talk of 'putting in a representative government'. Or, on the other hand, of 'restoring' the Kingdom to Afghanistan's 89-year old former King Zahir Shah, who has lived in exile in Rome since 1973. That's the way the game goes —support Saddam Hussein, then 'take him out'; finance the mujahideen, then bomb them to smithereens; put in Zahir Shah and see if he's going to be a good boy. (Is it possible to 'put in' a representative government? Can you place an order for Democracy – with extra cheese and jalapeno peppers?)

Reports have begun to trickle in about civilian casualties, about cities emptying out as Afghan civilians flock to the borders which have been closed. Main arterial roads have been blown up or sealed off. Those who have experience of working in Afghanistan say that by early November, food convoys will not be able to reach the millions of Afghans (7.5 million according to the UN) who run the very real risk of starving to death during the course of this winter. They say that in the days that are left before winter sets in, there can either be a war, or an attempt to reach food to the hungry. Not both.

As a gesture of humanitarian support, the US government air-dropped 37,000 packets of emergency rations into Afghanistan. It says it plans to drop a total of 500,000 packets. That will still only add up to a single meal for half a million people out of the several million in dire need of food. Aid workers have condemned it as a cynical, dangerous, public-relations exercise. They say that air-dropping food packets is worse than futile. First, because the food will never get to those who really need it. More dangerously, those who run out to retrieve the packets risk being blown up by land mines. A tragic alms race.

Nevertheless, the food packets had a photo-op all to themselves. Their contents were listed in major newspapers. They were vegetarian, we're told, as per Muslim Dietary Law (!) Each yellow packet, decorated with the American flag, contained: rice, peanut butter, bean salad, strawberry jam, crackers, raisins, flat bread, an apple fruit bar, seasoning, matches, a set of plastic cutlery, a serviette and illustrated user instructions.

After three years of unremitting drought, an air-dropped airline meal in Jalalabad! The level of cultural ineptitude, the failure to understand what months of relentless hunger and grinding poverty really mean, the US government's attempt to use even this abject misery to boost its self-image, beggars description.

Reverse the scenario for a moment. Imagine if the Taliban government was to bomb New York City, saying all the while that its real target was the US government and its policies. And suppose, during breaks between the bombing, the Taliban dropped a few thousand packets containing nan and kebabs impaled on an Afghan flag. Would the good people of New York ever find it in themselves to forgive the Afghan government? Even if they were hungry, even if they needed the food, even if they ate it, how would they ever forget the insult, the condescension? Rudi Guiliani, Mayor of New York City, returned a gift of $10 million from a Saudi prince because it came with a few words of friendly advice about American policy in the Middle East. Is pride a luxury that only the rich are entitled to?

Far from stamping it out, igniting this kind of rage is what creates terrorism. Hate and retribution don't go back into the box once you've let them out. For every 'terrorist' or his 'supporter' that is killed, hundreds of innocent people are being killed too. And for every hundred innocent people killed, there is a good chance that several future terrorists will be created.

Where will it all lead?

Setting aside the rhetoric for a moment, consider the fact that the world has not yet found an acceptable definition of what 'terrorism' is. One country's terrorist is too often another's freedom fighter. At the heart of the matter lies the world's deep-seated ambivalence towards violence. Once violence is accepted as a legitimate political instrument, then the morality and political acceptability of terrorists (insurgents or freedom fighters) becomes contentious, bumpy terrain. The US government itself has funded, armed and sheltered plenty of rebels and insurgents around the world. The CIA and Pakistan's ISI trained and armed the mujahideen who, in the eighties, were seen as terrorists by the government in Soviet-occupied Afghanistan. Today, Pakistan —America's ally in this new war – sponsors insurgents who cross the border into Kashmir in India. Pakistan lauds them as 'freedom-fighters', India calls them 'terrorists'. India, for its part, denounces countries who sponsor and abet terrorism, but the Indian army has, in the past, trained separatist Tamil rebels asking for a homeland in Sri Lanka – the LTTE, responsible for countless acts of bloody terrorism. (Just as the CIA abandoned the mujahideen after they had served its purpose, India abruptly turned its back on the LTTE for a host of political reasons. It was an enraged LTTE suicide bomber who assassinated former Indian Prime Rajiv Gandhi in 1989.)

It is important for governments and politicians to understand that manipulating these huge, raging human feelings for their own narrow purposes may yield instant results, but eventually and inexorably, they have disastrous consequences. Igniting and exploiting religious sentiments for reasons of political expediency is the most dangerous legacy that governments or politicians can bequeath to any people – including their own. People who live in societies ravaged by religious or communal bigotry know that every religious text – from the Bible to the Bhagwad Gita – can be mined and misinterpreted to justify anything, from nuclear war to genocide to corporate globalisation.

This is not to suggest that the terrorists who perpetrated the outrage on September 11th should not be hunted down and brought to book. They must be. But is war the best way to track them down? Will burning the haystack find you the needle? Or will it escalate the anger and make the world a living hell for all of us?

At the end of the day, how many people can you spy on, how many bank accounts can you freeze, how many conversations can you eavesdrop on, how many e-mails can you intercept, how many letters can you open, how many phones can you tap? Even before September 11th, the CIA had accumulated more information than is humanly possible to process. (Sometimes, too much data can actually hinder intelligence – small wonder the US spy satellites completely missed the preparation that preceded India's nuclear tests in 1998.)

The sheer scale of the surveillance will become a logistical, ethical and civil rights nightmare. It will drive everybody clean crazy. And freedom – that precious, precious thing – will be the first casualty. It's already hurt and haemorrhaging dangerously.

Governments across the world are cynically using the prevailing paranoia to promote their own interests. All kinds of unpredictable political forces are being unleashed. In India, for instance, members of the All India People's Resistance Forum, who were distributing anti-war and anti-US pamphlets in Delhi, have been jailed. Even the printer of the leaflets was arrested. The right-wing government (while it shelters Hindu extremists groups like the Vishwa Hindu Parishad and the Bajrang Dal) has banned the Students' Islamic Movement of India and is trying to revive an anti-terrorist Act which had been withdrawn after the Human Rights Commission reported that it had been more abused than used. Millions of Indian citizens are Muslim. Can anything be gained by alienating them?

Every day that the war goes on, raging emotions are being let loose into the world. The international press has little or no independent access to the war zone. In any case, mainstream media, particularly in the US, has more or less rolled over, allowing itself to be tickled on the stomach with press hand-outs from military men and government officials. Afghan radio stations have been destroyed by the bombing. The Taliban has always been deeply suspicious of the Press. In the propaganda war, there is no accurate estimate of how many people have been killed, or how much destruction has taken place. In the absence of reliable information, wild rumours spread.

Put your ear to the ground in this part of the world, and you can hear the thrumming, the deadly drumbeat of burgeoning anger. Please. Please, stop the war now. Enough people have died. The smart missiles are just not smart enough. They're blowing up whole warehouses of suppressed fury.

President George Bush recently boasted, 'When I take action, I'm not going to fire a $2 million missile at a $10 empty tent and hit a camel in the butt. It's going to be decisive.' President Bush should know that there are no targets in Afghanistan that will give his missiles their money's worth. Perhaps, if only to balance his books, he should develop some cheaper missiles to use on cheaper targets and cheaper lives in the poor countries of the world. But then, that may not make good business sense to the Coalition's weapons manufacturers. It wouldn't make any sense at all, for example, to the Carlyle Group – described by the Industry Standard as 'the world's largest private equity firm,' with $13 billion under management. Carlyle invests in the defence sector and makes its money from military conflicts and weapons spending.

Carlyle is run by men with impeccable credentials. Former US Defence Secretary Frank Carlucci is Carlyle's Chairman and Managing Director (he was a college roommate of Donald Rumsfeld's). Carlyle's other partners include former US Secretary of State James A. Baker III, George Soros, and Fred Malek (George Bush Sr's campaign manager). An American paper, the *Baltimore Chronicle and Sentinel*, says that former President George Bush Sr is reported to be seeking investments for the Carlyle Group from Asian markets. He is reportedly paid not inconsiderable sums of money to make 'presentations' to potential government-clients.

Ho Hum. As the tired saying goes, it's all in the family.

Then there's that other branch of traditional family business – oil. Remember, President George Bush (Jr) and Vice-President Dick Cheney both made their fortunes working in the US oil industry.

Turkmenistan, which borders the north-west of Afghanistan, holds the world's third largest gas reserves and an estimated six billion barrels of oil reserves. Enough, experts say, to meet American energy needs for the next thirty years (or a developing country's energy requirements for a couple of centuries.) America has always viewed oil as a security consideration, and protected it by any means it deems necessary. Few of us doubt that its military presence in the Gulf has little to do with its concern for human rights and is almost entirely to do with its strategic interest in oil.

Oil and gas from the Caspian region currently moves northward to European markets. Geographically and politically, Iran and Russia are major impediments to American interests. In 1998, Dick Cheney – then CEO of Halliburton, a major player in the oil industry – said, 'I can't think of a time when we've had a region emerge as suddenly to become as strategically significant as the Caspian. It's almost as if the opportunities have arisen overnight.' True enough.

For some years now, an American oil giant called Unocal has been negotiating with the Taliban for permission to construct an oil pipeline through Afghanistan to Pakistan and out to the Arabian Sea. From here, Unocal hopes to access the lucrative 'emerging markets' in South and South-east Asia. In December 1997, a delegation of Taliban mullahs travelled to America and even met US State Department officials and Unocal executives in Houston. At that time the Taliban's taste for public executions and its treatment of Afghan women were not made out to be the crimes against humanity that they are now. Over the next six months, pressure from hundreds of outraged American feminist groups was brought to bear on the Clinton Administration. Fortunately, they managed to scuttle the deal. And now comes the US oil industry's big chance.

In America, the arms industry, the oil industry, the major media networks, and, indeed, US foreign policy, are all controlled by the same business combines. Therefore, it would be foolish to expect this talk of guns and oil and defence deals to get any real play in the media. In any case, to a distraught, confused people whose pride has just been wounded, whose loved ones have been tragically killed, whose anger is fresh and sharp, the inanities about the 'Clash of Civilizations' and the 'Good versus Evil' discourse home in unerringly. They are cynically doled out by government spokesmen like a daily dose of vitamins or anti-depressants. Regular medication ensures that mainland America continues to remain the enigma it has always been – a curiously insular people, administered by a pathologically meddlesome, promiscuous government.

And what of the rest of us, the numb recipients of this onslaught of what we know to be preposterous propaganda? The daily consumers of the lies and brutality smeared in peanut butter and strawberry jam being air-dropped into our minds just like those yellow food packets. Shall we look away and eat because we're hungry, or shall we stare unblinking at the grim theatre unfolding in Afghanistan until we retch collectively and say, in one voice, that we have had enough?

As the first year of the new millennium rushes to a close, one wonders – have we forfeited our right to dream? Will we ever be able to re-imagine beauty? Will it be possible ever again to watch the slow, amazed blink of a new-born gecko in the sun, or whisper back to the marmot who has just whispered in your ear – without thinking of the World Trade Centre and Afghanistan?

The new war on terror

Noam Chomsky

Everyone knows it's the TV people who run the world [crowd laughter]. I just got orders that I'm supposed to be here, not there. Well the last talk I gave at this forum was on a light pleasant topic. It was about how humans are an endangered species and given the nature of their institutions they are likely to destroy themselves in a fairly short time. So this time there is a little relief and we have a pleasant topic instead, the new war on terror. Unfortunately, the world keeps coming up with things that make it more and more horrible as we proceed.

I'm going to assume two conditions for this talk.

- The first one is just what I assume to be recognition of fact. That is that the events of September 11th were a horrendous atrocity, probably the most devastating instant human toll of any crime in history, outside of war.
- The second assumption has to do with the goals. I'm assuming that our goal is that we are interested in reducing the likelihood of such crimes whether they are against us or against someone else.

If you don't accept those two assumptions, then what I say will not be addressed to you. If we do accept them, then a number of questions arise, closely related ones, which merit a good deal of thought.

The five questions

One question, and by far the most important one is what is happening right now? Implicit in that is what can we do about it? The second has to do with the very common assumption that what happened on September 11th is a historic event, one which will change history. I tend to agree with that. I think it's true. It was a historic event and the question we should be asking is exactly why? The third question has to do with the title, 'The War Against Terrorism'. Exactly what is it? And there is a related question, namely what is terrorism? The fourth question

Noam Chomsky is Professor of Linguistics at the Massachusetts Institute of Technology. This lecture was originally given on October 18, 2001, under the sponsorship of MIT's Technology & Culture Forum.

which is narrower but important has to do with the origins of the crimes of September 11th. And the fifth question that I want to talk a little about is what policy options there are in fighting this war against terrorism and dealing with the situations that led to it.

I'll say a few things about each. Glad to go beyond in discussion and don't hesitate to bring up other questions. These are ones that come to my mind as prominent but you may easily and plausibly have other choices.

I
What's happening right now?

Starvation of three to four million people

Well let's start with right now. I'll talk about the situation in Afghanistan. I'll just keep to uncontroversial sources like the *New York Times*. According to the *New York Times* there are seven to eight million people in Afghanistan on the verge of starvation. That was true actually before September 11th. They were surviving on international aid. On September 16th, the *Times* reported, I'm quoting it, that the United States demanded from Pakistan the elimination of truck convoys that provide much of the food and other supplies to Afghanistan's civilian population. As far as I could determine there was no reaction in the United States or for that matter in Europe. I was on national radio all over Europe the next day. There was no reaction in the United States or in Europe to my knowledge to the demand to impose massive starvation on millions of people. The threat of military strikes right after September 11th forced the removal of international aid workers that crippled the assistance programmes. Actually, I am quoting again from the *New York Times*. 'Refugees reaching Pakistan after arduous journeys from Afghanistan are describing scenes of desperation and fear at home as the threat of American led military attacks turns their long running misery into a potential catastrophe. The country was on a lifeline and we just cut the line', quoting an evacuated aid worker, in the *New York Times* Magazine.

The World Food Programme, the UN programme, which is the main one by far, was able to resume after three weeks in early October, when they began to resume at a lower level, resume food shipments. They don't have international aid workers within, so the distribution system is hampered. That was suspended as soon as the bombing began. They then resumed but at a lower pace while aid agencies levelled scathing condemnations of US airdrops, condemning them as propaganda tools which are probably doing more harm than good. That happens to be quoting the London *Financial Times* but it is easy to continue. After the first week of bombing, the *New York Times* reported on a back page inside a column on something else, that by the arithmetic of the United Nations there will soon be 7.5 million Afghans in acute need of even a loaf of bread and there are only a few weeks left before the harsh winter will make deliveries to many areas totally impossible, but with bombs falling the delivery rate is down to half of what is needed. Casual comment. Which tells us that Western civilization is anticipating the slaughter of three to four million people or something like that. On the same day, the leader of Western civilization dismissed with contempt, once again, offers of negotiation for delivery of the alleged target, Osama bin Laden, and a request for some evidence to substantiate the demand for total capitulation. It was dismissed. On the same day the Special Rapporteur of the United Nations in charge of food pleaded with the United States to stop the bombing to try to save millions of victims. As far as I'm aware that was unreported. The major aid agencies OXFAM and Christian Aid and others joined in that plea. You can't find a report in the *New York Times*. There was a line in the *Boston Globe*, hidden in a story about another topic, Kashmir.

Silent genocide

Well we could easily go on…but all of that…first of all indicates to us what's happening. Looks like what's happening is some sort of silent genocide. It also gives a good deal of insight into the elite culture, the culture that we are part of. It indicates that whatever, what will happen we don't know, but plans are being made and programmes implemented on the assumption that they may lead to the death of several million people in the next few months…very casually with no comment, no particular thought about it, that's just kind of normal, here and in a good part of Europe. Not in the rest of the world. In fact not even in much of Europe. So if you read the Irish press or the press in Scotland…that close, reactions are very different. Well that's what's happening now. What's happening now is very much under our control. We can do a lot to affect what's happening. And that's roughly it.

II
Why was it a historic event?

National territory attacked

Let's turn to the slightly more abstract question, forgetting for the moment that we are in the midst of apparently trying to murder three or four million people, not Taliban of course, their victims. Let's go back…turn to the question of the historic event that took place on September 11th. As I said, I think that's correct. It was a historic event. Not unfortunately because of its scale, unpleasant to think about, but in terms of the scale it's not that unusual. I did say it's the worst… probably the worst instant human toll of any crime. And that may be true. But there are terrorist crimes with effects a bit more drawn out that are more extreme, unfortunately. Nevertheless, it's a historic event because there was a change. The change was the direction in which the guns were pointed. That's new. Radically new. So, take US history.

The last time that the national territory of the United States was under attack, or for that matter even threatened, was when the British burned down Washington in 1814. There have been many…it was common to bring up Pearl Harbor but that's not a good analogy. The Japanese, whatever you think about it, the Japanese bombed military bases in two US colonies not the national territory; colonies which had been taken from their inhabitants in not a very pretty way.

This is the national territory that's been attacked on a large scale. You can find a few fringe examples but this is unique.

During these close to 200 years, we, the United States expelled or mostly exterminated the indigenous population, that's many millions of people, conquered half of Mexico, carried out depredations all over the region, Caribbean and Central America, sometimes beyond, conquered Hawaii and the Philippines, killing several hundreds of thousands of Filipinos in the process. Since the Second World War, it has extended its reach around the world in ways I don't have to describe. But it was always killing someone else, the fighting was somewhere else, it was others who were getting slaughtered. Not here. Not the national territory.

Europe

In the case of Europe, the change is even more dramatic because its history is even more horrendous than ours. We are an offshoot of Europe, basically. For hundreds of years, Europe has been casually slaughtering people all over the world. That's how they conquered the world, not by handing out candy to babies. During this period, Europe did suffer murderous wars, but that was European killers murdering one another. The main sport of Europe for hundreds of years was slaughtering one another. The only reason that it came to an end in 1945 had nothing to do with democracy or not making war with each other and other fashionable notions. It had to do with the fact that everyone understood that the next time they play the game it was going to be the end for the world. Because the Europeans, including us, had developed such massive weapons of destruction that that game just had to be over. And it goes back hundreds of years. In the 17th century, about probably 40% of the entire population of Germany was wiped out in one war.

But during this whole bloody murderous period, it was Europeans slaughtering each other, and Europeans slaughtering people elsewhere. The Congo didn't attack Belgium, India didn't attack England, Algeria didn't attack France. It's uniform. There are again small exceptions, but pretty small in scale, certainly invisible in the scale of what Europe and us were doing to the rest of the world. This is the first change. The first time that the guns have been pointed the other way. And in my opinion that's probably why you see such different reactions on the two sides of the Irish Sea which I have noticed, incidentally, in many interviews on both sides, national radio on both sides. The world looks very different depending on whether you are holding the lash or whether you are being whipped by it for hundreds of years, very different. So I think the shock and surprise in Europe and its offshoots, like here, is very understandable. It is a historic event but regrettably not in scale, in something else and a reason why most of the rest of the world looks at it quite differently. Not lacking sympathy for the victims of the atrocity or being horrified at them, that's almost uniform, but viewing it from a different perspective. Something we might want to understand.

III
What is the war against terrorism?

Let's go to the third question, 'What is the war against terrorism?' and a side question, 'What's terrorism?'. The war against terrorism has been described in high places as a struggle against a plague, a cancer which is spread by barbarians, by 'depraved opponents of civilization itself.' That's a feeling that I share. The words I'm quoting, however, happen to be from 20 years ago. The Reagan Administration came into office 20 years ago declaring that the war against international terrorism would be the core of our foreign policy describing it in terms of the kind I just mentioned and others. And it was the core of our foreign policy. The Reagan Administration responded to this plague spread by depraved opponents of civilization itself by creating an extraordinary international terrorist network, totally unprecedented in scale, which carried out massive atrocities all over the world.

Reagan-US war against Nicaragua

But I'll just mention one case which is totally uncontroversial, so we might as well not argue about it, by no means the most extreme but uncontroversial. It's uncontroversial because of the judgments of the highest international authorities the International Court of Justice, the World Court, and the UN Security Council. So this one is uncontroversial, at least among people who have some minimal concern for international law, human rights, justice and other things like that. And now I'll leave you an exercise. You can estimate the size of that category by simply asking how often this uncontroversial case has been mentioned in the commentary of the last month. And it's a particularly relevant one, not only because it is uncontroversial, but because it does offer a precedent as to how a law abiding state would respond to – did respond in fact to – international terrorism, which is uncontroversial. And was even more extreme than the events of September 11th. I'm talking about the Reagan-US war against Nicaragua which left tens of thousands of people dead, the country ruined, perhaps beyond recovery.

Nicaragua's response

Nicaragua did respond. They didn't respond by setting off bombs in Washington. They responded by taking it to the World Court, presenting a case, they had no problem putting together evidence. The World Court accepted their case, ruled in their favour, condemned what they called the 'unlawful use of force,' which is another word for international terrorism, by the United States, ordered the United States to terminate the crime and to pay massive reparations. The United States, of course, dismissed the court judgment with total contempt and announced that it would not accept the jurisdiction of the court henceforth. Nicaragua then went to the UN Security Council which considered a resolution calling on all states to observe international law. No one was mentioned but everyone understood. The United States vetoed the resolution. It now stands as the only state on record which has both been condemned by the World Court for international terrorism and has vetoed a Security Council resolution calling on states to observe international law. Nicaragua then went to the General Assembly where there is technically no veto but a negative US vote amounts to a veto. It passed a similar resolution with only the United States, Israel, and El Salvador opposed. The following year again, this time the United States could only rally Israel to the cause, so two votes opposed to observing international law. At that point, Nicaragua couldn't do anything lawful. It had tried all the measures. They don't work in a world that is ruled by force.

This case is uncontroversial but it's by no means the most extreme. We gain a lot of insight into our own culture and society and what's happening now by asking 'how much we know about all this? How much we talk about it? How much you learn about it in school? How much it's all over the front pages?' And this is only the beginning. The United States responded to the World Court and the Security Council by immediately escalating the war very quickly. That was a bipartisan decision incidentally. The terms of the war were also changed. For the first time there were official orders given…official orders to the terrorist army to attack what are called 'soft targets,' meaning undefended civilian targets, and to keep away from the Nicaraguan army. They were able to do that because the United States had total control of the air over Nicaragua and the mercenary army was supplied with advanced communication equipment. It wasn't a guerrilla army in the normal sense and could get instructions about the disposition of the Nicaraguan army forces so they could attack agricultural collectives, health clinics, and so on – soft targets – with impunity. Those were the official orders.

What was the reaction here?

What was the reaction? It was known. There was a reaction to it. The policy was regarded as sensible by left liberal opinion. So Michael Kinsley who represents the left in mainstream discussion, wrote an article in which he said that we shouldn't be too quick to criticize this policy as Human Rights Watch had just done. He said a 'sensible policy' must 'meet the test of cost benefit analysis' – that is, I'm quoting now, that is the analysis of 'the amount of blood and misery that will be poured in, and the likelihood that democracy will emerge at the other end.' Democracy as the US understands the term, which is graphically illustrated in the surrounding countries. Notice that it is axiomatic that the United States, US elites, have the right to conduct the analysis and to pursue the project if it passes their tests. And it did pass their tests. It worked. When Nicaragua finally succumbed to superpower assault, commentators openly and cheerfully lauded the success of the methods that were adopted and described them accurately. So I'll quote *Time Magazine* just to pick one. They lauded the success of the methods adopted: 'to wreck the economy and prosecute a long and deadly proxy war until the exhausted natives overthrow the unwanted government themselves,' with a cost to us that is 'minimal,' and leaving the victims 'with wrecked bridges, sabotaged power stations, and ruined farms,' and thus providing the US candidate with a 'winning issue': 'ending the impoverishment of the people of Nicaragua.' The *New York Times* had a headline saying 'Americans United in Joy' at this outcome.

Terrorism works – terrorism is not the weapon of the weak

That is the culture in which we live and it reveals several facts. One is the fact that terrorism works. It doesn't fail. It works. Violence usually works. That's world history. Secondly, it's a very serious analytic error to say, as is commonly done, that terrorism is the weapon of the weak. Like other means of violence, it's primarily a weapon of the strong, overwhelmingly, in fact. It is held to be a weapon of the weak because the strong also control the doctrinal systems and their terror doesn't count as terror. Now that's close to universal. I can't think of a historical exception, even the worst mass murderers view the world that way. So pick the Nazis. They weren't carrying out terror in occupied Europe. They were protecting the local population from the terrorisms of the partisans. And as with other resistance movements, there was terrorism. The Nazis were carrying out counter-terror. Furthermore, the United States essentially agreed with that. After the war, the US army did extensive studies of Nazi counter-terror operations in Europe. First I should say that the US picked them up and began carrying them out itself, often against the same targets, the former resistance. But the military also studied the Nazi methods and published interesting studies, sometimes critical of them because they were inefficiently carried out, so a critical analysis, you didn't do this right, you did that right. But those methods, with the advice of *Wehrmacht* officers who were brought over here, became the manuals of counter-insurgency, of counter-terror, of low intensity conflict, as it is called, and are the manuals, and are the procedures that are being used. So it's not just that the Nazis did it. It's that it was regarded as the right thing to do by the leaders of western civilization, that is us, who then proceeded to do it themselves. Terrorism is not the weapon of the weak. It is the weapon of those who are against 'us' whoever 'us' happens to be. And if you can find a historical exception to that, I'd be interested in seeing it.

Nature of our culture – how we regard terrorism

An interesting indication of the nature of our culture, our high culture, is the way in which all of this is regarded. One way it's regarded is just suppressing it. So almost nobody has ever heard of it. And the power of American propaganda and doctrine is so strong that even among the victims it's barely known. I mean, when you talk about this to people in Argentina, you have to remind them. Oh, yes, that happened, we forgot about it. It's deeply suppressed. The sheer consequences of the monopoly of violence can be very powerful in ideological and other terms.

The idea that Nicaragua might have the right to defend itself

One illuminating aspect of our own attitude towards terrorism is the reaction to the idea that Nicaragua might have the right to defend itself. Actually I went through this in some detail with database searches and that sort of thing. The idea that Nicaragua might have the right to defend itself was considered outrageous. There is virtually nothing in mainstream commentary indicating that Nicaragua might have that right. And that fact was exploited by the Reagan Administration and its propaganda in an interesting way. Those of you who were around in that time will remember that they periodically floated rumours that the Nicaraguans were getting MIG jets from Russia. At that point the hawks and the doves split. The hawks said, 'ok, let's bomb 'em.' The doves said, 'wait a minute, let's see if the rumours are true. And if the rumours are true, then let's bomb them. Because they are a threat to the United States.' Why, incidentally, were they getting MIGs? They tried to get jet planes from European countries but the United States put pressure on its allies so that it wouldn't send them means of defence because they *wanted* them to turn to the Russians. That's good for propaganda purposes. Then they become a threat to us. Remember, they were just two days march from Harlingen, Texas. We actually declared a national emergency in 1985 to protect the country from the threat of Nicaragua. And it stayed in force. So it was much better for them to get arms from the Russians. Why would they want jet planes? Well, for the reasons I already mentioned. The United States had total control over their airspace, was over-flying it and using that to provide instructions to the terrorist army to enable them to attack soft targets without running into the army that might defend them. Everyone knew that that was the reason. They are not going to use their jet planes for anything else. But the idea that Nicaragua should be permitted to defend its airspace against a superpower attack that is directing terrorist forces to attack undefended civilian targets, that was considered in the United States as outrageous and uniformly so. Exceptions are so slight, you know I can practically list them. I don't suggest that you take my word for this. Have a look. That includes our own senators, incidentally.

Honduras – The appointment of John Negroponte as Ambassador to the United Nations

Another illustration of how we regard terrorism is happening right now. The US has just appointed an ambassador to the United Nations to lead the war against terrorism a couple of weeks ago. Who is he? Well, his name is John Negroponte. He was the US Ambassador in the fiefdom, which is what it is, of Honduras in the early 1980s. There was a little fuss made about the fact that he must have been aware, as he certainly was, of the large-scale murders and other atrocities that were being carried out by the security forces in Honduras that we were supporting. But that's a small part of it. As proconsul of Honduras, as he was called there, he was the local supervisor for the terrorist war based in Honduras, for which his government was condemned by the world court and then the Security Council in a vetoed resolution. And this is the man who has just been appointed as the UN Ambassador to lead the war against terror. Now that tells us a lot about the war against terrorism and a lot about ourselves.

After the United States took over the country again under the conditions that were so graphically described by the press, the country was pretty much destroyed in the 1980s, but it has totally collapsed since just about in every respect. Economically it has declined sharply since the US take-over, democratically and in every other respect. It's now amongst the poorest countries in the Hemisphere.

US & UK backed South African attacks
It was happening elsewhere in the world too, take Africa, say. During the Reagan years alone, South African attacks, backed by the United States and Britain, against the neighbouring countries killed about a million and a half people and left 60 billion dollars in damage and countries destroyed. And if we go around the world, we can add more examples.

Now that was the first war against terror of which I've given a small sample. Are we supposed to pay attention to that? Or kind of think that that might be relevant? After all it's not exactly ancient history. Well, evidently not as you can tell by looking at the current discussion of the war on terror which has been the leading topic for the last month.

Haiti, Guatemala, and Nicaragua
Nicaragua has now become the second poorest country in the hemisphere. What's the poorest country? Well that's of course Haiti which also happens to be the victim of most US intervention in the 20th century by a long shot. We left it totally devastated. It's the poorest country. Nicaragua is second ranked in degree of US intervention in the 20th century. It is the second poorest. Actually, it is vying with Guatemala. They interchange every year or two as to who's the second poorest. And they also vie as to who is the leading target of US military intervention. We're supposed to think that all of this is some sort of accident. That is has nothing to do with anything that happened in history. Maybe.

Colombia and Turkey
The worst human rights violator in the 1990s is Colombia, by a long shot. It's also, by far, the leading recipient of US military aid in the 1990s maintaining the terror and human rights violations. In 1999, Colombia replaced Turkey as the leading recipient of US arms worldwide, that is excluding Israel and Egypt which are a separate category. And that tells us a lot more about the war on terror right now, in fact.

Why was Turkey getting such a huge flow of US arms? Well if you take a look at the flow of US arms to Turkey, Turkey always got a lot of US arms. It's strategically placed, a member of NATO, and so on. But the arms flow to Turkey went up very sharply in 1984. It didn't have anything to do with the Cold War. I mean Russia was collapsing. And it stayed high from 1984 to 1999 when it reduced and it was replaced in the lead by Colombia. What happened from 1984 to 1999? Well, in 1984, Turkey launched a major terrorist war against Kurds in southeastern Turkey. And that's when US aid went up, military aid. And this was not pistols. This was jet planes, tanks, military training, and so on. And it stayed high as the atrocities escalated through the 1990s. Aid followed it. The peak year was 1997. In 1997, US military aid to Turkey was more than in the entire period 1950 to 1983, that is the Cold War period, which is an indication of how much the Cold War has affected policy. And the results were awesome. This led to two to three million refugees and some of the worst ethnic cleansing of the late 1990s. Tens of thousands of people killed, 3500 towns and villages destroyed, way more than Kosovo, even under NATO bombs. And the United States was providing 80% of the arms, increasing as the atrocities increased, peaking in 1997. It declined in 1999 because, once again, terror worked as it usually does when carried out by its major agents, mainly the powerful. So by 1999, Turkish terror, called of course counter-terror, but as I said, that's universal, it worked. Therefore Turkey was replaced by Colombia which had not yet succeeded in its terrorist war. And therefore had to move into first place as recipient of US arms.

Self-congratulation on the part of Western intellectuals

What makes this all particularly striking is that all of this was taking place right in the midst of a huge flood of self-congratulation on the part of Western intellectuals which probably has no counterpart in history. You all remember it. It was just a couple years ago. Massive self-adulation about how for the first time in history we are so magnificent; that we are standing up for principles and values; dedicated to ending inhumanity everywhere in the new era of this-and-that, and so-on-and-so-forth. And we certainly can't tolerate atrocities right near the borders of NATO. That was repeated over and over. Only within the borders of NATO where we not only can tolerate much worse atrocities but also contribute to them. Another insight into Western civilization and our own, is how often was this brought up? Try to look. I won't repeat it. But it's instructive. It's a pretty impressive feat for a propaganda system to carry this off in a free society. It's pretty amazing. I don't think you could do this in a totalitarian state.

Turkey is very grateful

And Turkey is very grateful. Just a few days ago, Prime Minister Ecevit announced that Turkey would join the coalition against terror, very enthusiastically, even more so than others. In fact, he said they would contribute troops which others have not been willing to do. And he explained why. He said, We owe a debt of gratitude to the United States because the United States was the only country that was willing to contribute so massively to our own, in his words 'counter-terrorist' war, that is to our own massive ethnic cleansing and atrocities and terror. Other countries helped a little, but they stayed back. The United States, on the other hand, contributed enthusiastically and decisively and was able to do so because of the silence – servility might be the right word – of the educated classes who could easily find out about it. It's a free country after all. You can read human rights reports. You can read all sorts of stuff. But we chose to contribute to the atrocities and Turkey is very happy, they owe us a debt of gratitude for that and therefore will contribute troops just as during the war in Serbia. Turkey was very much praised for using its F-16s which we supplied to bomb Serbia exactly as it had been doing with the same planes against its own population up until the time when it finally succeeded in crushing internal terror as they called it. And as usual, as always, resistance does include terror. Its true of the American

Revolution. That's true of every case I know. Just as its true that those who have a monopoly of violence talk about themselves as carrying out counter-terror.

The coalition – including Algeria, Russia, China, Indonesia

Now that's pretty impressive and that has to do with the coalition that is now being organized to fight the war against terror. And it's very interesting to see how that coalition is being described. So have a look at this morning's *Christian Science Monitor*. That's a good newspaper. One of the best international newspapers, with real coverage of the world. The lead story, the front-page story, is about how the United States, you know people used to dislike the United States but now they are beginning to respect it, and they are very happy about the way that the US is leading the war against terror. And the prime example, well in fact the only serious example, the others are a joke, is Algeria. Turns out that Algeria is very enthusiastic about the US war against terror. The person who wrote the article is an expert on Africa. He must know that Algeria is one of the most vicious terrorist states in the world and has been carrying out horrendous terror against its own population in the past couple of years, in fact. For a while, this was under wraps. But it was finally exposed in France by defectors from the Algerian army. It's all over the place there and in England and so on. But here, we're very proud because one of the worst terrorist states in the world is now enthusiastically welcoming the US war on terror and in fact is cheering on the United States to lead the war. That shows how popular we are getting.

And if you look at the coalition that is being formed against terror it tells you a lot more. A leading member of the coalition is Russia which is delighted to have the United States support its murderous terrorist war in Chechnya instead of occasionally criticizing it in the background. China is joining enthusiastically. It's delighted to have support for the atrocities it's carrying out in western China against, what it called, Muslim secessionists. Turkey, as I mentioned, is very happy with the war against terror. They are experts. Algeria, Indonesia delighted to have even more US support for atrocities it is carrying out in Aceh and elsewhere. Now we can run through the list, the list of the states that have joined the coalition against terror is quite impressive. They have a characteristic in common. They are certainly among the leading terrorist states in the world. And they happen to be led by the world champion.

What is terrorism?

That brings us back to the question, what is terrorism? I have been assuming we understand it. What is it? Well, there happen to be some easy answers to this. There is an official definition. You can find it in the US code or in US army manuals. A brief statement of it taken from a US army manual is that terror is the calculated use of violence or the threat of violence to attain political or religious ideological goals through intimidation, coercion, or instilling fear. That's terrorism. That's a fair enough definition. I think it is reasonable to accept that. The problem is that it can't be accepted because if you accept that, all the wrong consequences follow. For example, all the consequences I have just been reviewing. There is a major effort right now at the UN to try to develop a comprehensive treaty on terrorism. When Kofi Annan got the Nobel prize the other day, you will notice he was reported as saying that we should stop wasting time on this and really get down to it.

But there's a problem. If you use the official definition of terrorism in the comprehensive treaty you are going to get completely the wrong results. So that can't be done. In fact, it is even worse than that. If you take a look at the definition of Low Intensity Warfare which is official US policy you find that it is a very close paraphrase of what I just read. In fact, Low Intensity Conflict is just another name for terrorism. That's why all countries, as far as I know, call whatever horrendous acts they are carrying out, counter-terrorism. We happen to call it Counter Insurgency or Low Intensity Conflict. So that's a serious problem. You can't use the actual definitions. You've got to carefully find a definition that doesn't have all the wrong consequences.

Why did the United States and Israel vote against a major resolution condemning terrorism?

There are some other problems. Some of them came up in December 1987, at the peak of the first war on terrorism. That's when the furore over the plague was peaking. The United Nations General Assembly passed a very strong resolution against terrorism, condemning the plague in the strongest terms, calling on every state to fight against it in every possible way. It passed unanimously. One country, Honduras abstained. Two votes against; the usual two, United States and Israel. Why should the United States and Israel vote against a major resolution condemning terrorism in the strongest terms, in fact pretty much the terms that the Reagan administration was using? Well, there is a reason. There is one paragraph in that long resolution which says that nothing in this resolution infringes on the rights of people struggling against racist and colonialist regimes or foreign military occupation to continue with their resistance with the assistance of others, other states, states outside in their just cause. Well, the United States and Israel can't accept that. The main reason that they couldn't at the time was because of South Africa. South Africa was an ally, officially called an ally. There was a terrorist force in South Africa. It was called the African National Congress. They were a terrorist force officially. South Africa in contrast was an ally and we certainly couldn't support actions by a terrorist group struggling against a racist regime. That would be impossible.

And of course there is another one. Namely the Israeli occupied territories, now going into its 35th year. Supported primarily by the United States in blocking a diplomatic settlement for 30 years now, still is. And you can't have that. There is another one at the time. Israel was occupying Southern Lebanon and was being combated by what the US calls a terrorist force, Hizbullah, which in fact succeeded in driving Israel out of Lebanon. And we can't allow anyone to struggle against a military occupation when it is one that we support so therefore the US and Israel had to vote against the major UN resolution on terrorism. And I mentioned before that a US vote against is essentially a veto. Which is only half the story. It also vetoes it from history. So none of this was ever reported and none of it appeared in the annals of terrorism. If you look at the scholarly work on terrorism and so on, nothing that I just mentioned appears. The reason is that it has got the wrong people holding the guns. You have to carefully hone the definitions and the scholarship and so on so that you come out with the right conclusions; otherwise it is not respectable scholarship and honourable journalism. These are some of problems that are hampering the effort to develop a comprehensive treaty against terrorism. Maybe we should have an academic conference or something to try to see if we can figure out a way of defining terrorism so that it comes out with just the right answers, not the wrong answers. That won't be easy.

IV
What are the origins of the September 11th crime?

Well, let's drop that and turn to the 4th question, What are the origins of the September 11 crimes? Here we have to make a distinction between two categories which shouldn't be run together. One is the actual agents of the crime, the other is kind of a reservoir of at least sympathy, sometimes support that they appeal to even among people who very much oppose the criminals and the actions. And those are two different things.

Category one: the likely perpetrators

With regard to the perpetrators, in a certain sense we are not really clear. The United States either is unable or unwilling to provide any evidence, any meaningful evidence. There was a sort of a play a week or two ago when Tony Blair was set up to try to present it. I don't exactly know what the purpose of this was. Maybe so that the US could look as though it's holding back on some secret evidence that it can't reveal or that Tony Blair could strike proper Churchillian poses or something or other. Whatever the public relations reasons were, he gave a presentation which was in serious circles considered so absurd that it was barely even mentioned. So the *Wall Street Journal*, for example, one of the more serious papers had a small story on page 12, I think, in which they pointed out that there was not much evidence and then they quoted some high US official as saying that it didn't matter whether there was any evidence because they were going to do it anyway. So why bother with the evidence? The more ideological press, like the *New York Times* and others, had big front-page headlines. But the *Wall Street Journal* reaction was reasonable and if you look at the so-called evidence you can see why. But let's assume that it's true. It is astonishing to me how weak the evidence was. I sort of thought you could do better than that without any intelligence service. In fact, remember this was after weeks of the most intensive investigation in history of all the intelligence services of the western world working overtime trying to put something together. And it was a prima facie, it was a very strong case even before you had anything. And it ended up about where it started, with a prima-facie case. So let's assume that it is true. So let's assume that, it looked obvious the first day, still does, that the actual perpetrators come from the radical Islamic, here called, fundamentalist networks of which the bin Laden network is undoubtedly a significant part. Whether they were involved or not nobody knows. It doesn't really matter much.

Where did they come from?

That's the background, those networks. Where do they come from? We know all about that. Nobody knows about that better than the CIA because it helped organize them and it nurtured them for a long time. They were brought together in the 1980s actually by the CIA and its associates elsewhere: Pakistan, Britain, France, Saudi Arabia, Egypt. China was involved: they may have been involved a little bit earlier, maybe by 1978. The idea was to try to harass the Russians, the common enemy. According to President Carter's National Security Advisor, Zbigniew Brzezinski, the US got involved in mid 1979. Do you remember, just to put the dates right, that Russia invaded Afghanistan in December 1979. According to Brzezinski, the US support for the mojahedin fighting against the government began six months earlier. He is very proud of that. He says we drew the Russians into, in his words, an Afghan trap, by supporting the mojahedin, getting them to invade, getting them into the trap. Now then we could develop this terrific mercenary army. Not a small one, maybe 100,000 men or so bringing together the best killers they could find, who were radical Islamist fanatics from around North Africa, Saudi Arabia…anywhere they could find them. They were often called the Afghanis but many of them, like bin Laden, were not Afghans. They were brought by the CIA and its friends from elsewhere. Whether Brzezinski is telling the truth or not, I don't know. He may have been bragging, he is apparently very proud of it, knowing the consequences incidentally. But maybe it's true. We'll know someday if the documents are ever released. Anyway, that's his perception. By January 1980 it is not even in doubt that the US was organizing the Afghanis and this massive military force to try to cause the Russians maximal trouble. It was a legitimate thing for the Afghans to fight the Russian invasion. But the US intervention was not helping the Afghans. In fact, it helped destroy the country and much more. It did force the Russians to withdraw, finally. Although many analysts believe that it probably delayed their withdrawal because they were trying to get out of it. Anyway, they did withdraw.

Meanwhile, the terrorist forces that the CIA was organizing, arming, and training were pursuing their own agenda, right away. It was no secret. One of the first acts was in 1981 when they assassinated the President of Egypt, who was one of the most enthusiastic of their creators. In 1983, one suicide bomber, who may or may not have been connected – it's pretty shadowy, nobody knows – drove the US army-military out of Lebanon. And it continued. They have their own agenda. The US was happy to mobilize them to fight its cause but meanwhile they are doing their own thing. They were very clear about it. After 1989, when the Russians had withdrawn, they simply turned elsewhere. Since then they have been fighting in Chechnya, Western China, Bosnia, Kashmir, South East Asia, North Africa, all over the place.

The are telling us what they think

They are telling us just what they think. The United States wants to silence the one free television channel in the Arab world because it's broadcasting a whole range of things from Powell to Osama bin Laden. So the US is now joining the repressive regimes of the Arab world that try to shut it up. But if you listen to it, if you listen to what bin Laden says, it's worth it. There are plenty of interviews. And there are plenty of interviews by leading Western reporters, if you don't want to listen to his own voice, Robert Fisk and others. And what he has been saying is pretty consistent for a long time. He's not the only one but maybe he is the most eloquent. It's not only consistent over a long time, it is consistent with their actions. So there is every reason to take it seriously. Their prime enemy is what they call the corrupt and oppressive authoritarian brutal regimes of the Arab world and when the say that they get quite a resonance in the region. They also want to replace them by properly Islamist governments. That's where they lose the people of the region. But up till then, they are with them. From their point of view, even Saudi Arabia, the most extreme fundamentalist state in the world, I suppose, short of the Taliban, which is an offshoot, even that's not Islamist enough for them. At that point, they get very little support, but up until that point they get plenty of support. Also they want to defend Muslims elsewhere. They hate the Russians like poison, but as soon as the Russians pulled out of Afghanistan, they stopped carrying out terrorist acts in Russia as they had been doing with CIA backing before that within Russia, not just in Afghanistan. They did move over to Chechnya. But there they are defending Muslims against a Russian invasion. Same with all the other places I mentioned. From their point of view, they are defending the Muslims against the infidels. And they are very clear about it and that is what they have been doing.

Why did they turn against the United States?

Now why did they turn against the United States? Well that had to do with what they call the US invasion of Saudi Arabia. In 1990, the US established permanent military bases in Saudi Arabia which from their point of view is comparable to a Russian invasion of Afghanistan except that Saudi Arabia is way more important. That's the home of the holiest sites of Islam. And that is when their activities turned against the United States. If you recall, in 1993 they tried to blow up the World Trade Centre. The plans were to blow up the UN building, the Holland and Lincoln tunnels, the FBI building. I think there were others on the list. They got part way, but not all the way. One person who is jailed for that, finally, among the people who were jailed, was an Egyptian cleric who had been brought into the United States over the objections of the Immigration Service, thanks to the intervention of the CIA which wanted to help out their friend. A couple of years later he was blowing up the World Trade Centre. And this has been going on all over. I'm not going to run through the list but it's a consistent picture. It's described in words. It's revealed in practice for 20 years. There is no reason not to take it seriously. That's the first category, the likely perpetrators.

Category two: what about the reservoir of support?

What about the reservoir of support? Well, it's not hard to find out what that is. One of the good things that has happened since September 11 is that some of the press and some of the discussion has begun to open up to some of these things. The best one to my knowledge is the *Wall Street Journal* which right away began to run, within a couple of days, serious reports, searching serious reports, on the reasons why the people of the region, even though they hate bin Laden and despise everything he is doing, nevertheless support him in many ways and even regard him as the conscience of Islam, as one said. Now the *Wall Street Journal* and others are not surveying public opinion. They are surveying the opinion of their friends: bankers, professionals, international lawyers, businessmen tied to the United States, people who they interview in MacDonalds restaurant, which is an elegant restaurant there, wearing fancy American clothes. That's the people they are interviewing because they want to find out what their attitudes are. And their attitudes are very explicit and very clear and in many ways consonant with the message of bin Laden and others. They are very angry at the United States because of its support of authoritarian and brutal regimes; its intervention to block any move towards democracy; its intervention to stop economic development; its policies of devastating the civilian societies of Iraq while strengthening Saddam Hussein; and they remember, even if we prefer not to, that the United States and Britain supported Saddam Hussein right through his worst atrocities, including the gassing of the Kurds, bin Laden brings that up constantly, and they know it even if we don't want to. And of course their support for the Israeli military occupation which is harsh and brutal. It is now in its 35th year. The US has been providing the overwhelming economic, military, and diplomatic support for it, and still does. They know that and they don't like it. Especially when that is paired with US policy towards Iraq, towards the Iraqi civilian society which is getting destroyed. Those are the reasons roughly. And when bin Laden gives those reasons, people recognize it and support it.

Now that's not the way people here like to think about it, at least educated liberal opinion. They like the following line which has been all over the press, mostly from left liberals, incidentally. I have not done a real study but I think right wing opinion has generally been more honest. But if you look, say, at the *New York Times* at the first opinion piece they ran by Ronald Steel, serious left liberal intellectual. He asks: 'Why do they hate us?' This is the same day, I think, that the *Wall Street Journal* was running the survey on why they hate us. So he says 'They hate us because we champion a new world order of capitalism, individualism, secularism, and democracy that should be the norm everywhere.' That's why they hate us. The same day the *Wall Street Journal* is surveying the opinions of bankers, professionals, international lawyers and saying 'look, we hate you because you are blocking democracy, you are preventing economic development, you are supporting brutal regimes, terrorist regimes and you are doing these horrible things in the region.' A couple of days later, Anthony Lewis, way out on the left, explained that the terrorist seek only 'apocalyptic nihilism,' nothing more and nothing we do matters. The only consequence of our actions, he says, that could be harmful is that it makes it harder for Arabs to join in the coalition's anti-terrorism effort. But beyond that, everything we do is irrelevant.

Well, you know, that's got the advantage of being sort of comforting. It makes you feel good about yourself, and how wonderful you are. It enables us to evade the consequences of our actions. It has a couple of defects. One is it is at total variance with everything we know. And another defect is that it is a perfect way to ensure that you escalate the cycle of violence. If you want to live with your head buried in the sand and pretend they hate us because they're opposed to globalization, that's why they killed Sadat 20 years ago, and fought the Russians, tried to blow up the World Trade Centre in 1993. And these are all people who are in the midst of corporate globalization but if you want to believe that, yes it's comforting. And it is a great way to make sure that violence escalates. That's tribal violence. You did something to me, I'll do something worse to you. I don't care what the reasons are. We just keep going that way. And that's a way to do it. Pretty much straight, left-liberal opinion.

V
What are the policy options?

What are the policy options? Well, there are a number. A narrow policy option from the beginning was to follow the advice of really far-out radicals like the Pope. The Vatican immediately said look it's a horrible terrorist crime. In the case of crime, you try to find the perpetrators, you bring them to justice, you try them. You don't kill innocent civilians. Like if somebody robs my house and I think the guy who did it is probably in the neighbourhood across the street, I don't go out with an assault rifle and kill everyone in that neighbourhood. That's not the way you deal with crime, whether it's a small crime like this one or really massive one like the US terrorist war against Nicaragua, even worse ones and others in between. And there are plenty of precedents for that. In fact, I mentioned a precedent, Nicaragua, a lawful, a law abiding state, (that's why presumably we had to destroy it) which followed the right principles. Now of course, it didn't get anywhere because it was running up against a power that wouldn't allow lawful procedures to be followed. But if the United States tried to pursue them, nobody would stop them. In fact, everyone would applaud. And there are plenty of other precedents.

IRA bombs in London

When the IRA set off bombs in London, which is pretty serious business, one possible response for Britain would have been to destroy Boston which is the source of most of the financing. And of course to wipe out West Belfast. Well, you know, quite apart from the feasibility, it would have been criminal idiocy. The way to deal with it was pretty much what they did: find the perpetrators; bring them to trial; and look for the reasons. Because these things don't come out of nowhere. They come from something. Whether it is a crime in the streets or a monstrous terrorist crime or anything else. There's reasons. And usually if you look at the reasons, some of them are legitimate and ought to be addressed, independently of the crime, they ought to be addressed because they are legitimate. And that's the way to deal with it. There are many such examples.

But there are problems with that. One problem is that the United States does not recognize the jurisdiction of international institutions. So it can't go to them. It has rejected the jurisdiction of the World Court. It has refused to ratify the International Criminal Court. It is powerful enough to set up a new court if it wants so that wouldn't stop anything. But there is a problem with any kind of a court, mainly you need evidence. You go to any kind of court, you need some kind of evidence. Not Tony Blair talking about it on television. And that's very hard. It may be impossible to find.

Leaderless resistance

You know, it could be that the people who did it, killed themselves. Nobody knows this better than the CIA. These are decentralized, non-hierarchic networks. They follow a principle that is called Leaderless Resistance. That's the principle that has been developed by the Christian Right terrorists in the United States. It's called Leaderless Resistance. You have small groups that do things. They don't talk to anybody else. There is a kind of general background of assumptions and then you do it. Actually people in the anti-war movement are very familiar with it. We used to call it affinity groups. If you assume correctly that whatever group you are in is being penetrated by the FBI, when something serious is happening, you don't do it in a meeting. You do it with some people you know and trust, an affinity group, and then it doesn't get penetrated. That's one of the reasons why the FBI has never been able to figure out what's going on in any of the popular movements. And other intelligence agencies are the same. They can't. That's leaderless resistance or affinity groups, and decentralized networks are extremely hard to penetrate. And it's quite possible that they just don't know. When Osama bin Laden claims he wasn't involved, that's entirely possible. In fact, it's pretty hard to imagine how a guy in a cave in Afghanistan, who doesn't even have a radio or a telephone, could have planned a highly sophisticated operation like that. Chances are it's part of the background. You know, like other leaderless resistance terrorist groups. Which means it's going to be extremely difficult to find evidence.

Establishing credibility

And the US doesn't want to present evidence because it wants to be able to act without evidence. That's a crucial part of the reaction. You will notice that the US did not ask for Security Council authorization which they probably could have gotten this time, not for pretty reasons, but because the other permanent members of the Security Council are also terrorist states. They are happy to join a coalition against what they call terror, namely in support of their own terror. Like Russia wasn't going to veto, they love it. So the US probably could have gotten Security Council authorization but it didn't want it. And it didn't want it because it follows a long-standing principle which does not originate with George Bush. It was explicit in the Clinton Administration, articulated and goes back much further and that is that we have the right to act unilaterally. We don't want international authorization because we act unilaterally and therefore we don't want it. We don't care about evidence. We don't care about negotiation. We don't care about treaties. We are the strongest guy around; the toughest thug on the block. We do what we want. Authorization is a bad thing and therefore must be avoided. There is even a name for it in the technical literature. It's called establishing credibility. You have to establish credibility. That's an important factor in many policies. It was the official reason given for the war in the Balkans and the most plausible reason.

You want to know what credibility means, ask your favourite Mafia Don. He'll explain to you what credibility means. And it's the same in international affairs, except it's talked about in universities using big words, and that sort of thing. But it's basically the same principle. And it makes sense. And it usually works. The main historian who has written about this in the last couple years is Charles Tilly with a book called *Coercion, Capital, and European States*. He points out that violence has been the leading principle of Europe for hundreds of years and the reason is because it works. You know, it's very reasonable. It almost always works. When you have an overwhelming predominance of violence and a culture of violence behind it. So therefore it makes sense to follow it. Well, those are all problems in pursuing lawful paths. And if you did try to follow them you'd really open some very dangerous doors. Like the US is demanding that the Taliban hand over Osama bin Laden. And they are responding in a way which is regarded as totally absurd and outlandish in the West, namely they are saying, OK, but first give us some evidence. In the West, that is considered ludicrous. It's a sign of their criminality. How can they ask for evidence? I mean if somebody asked us to hand someone over, we'd do it tomorrow. We wouldn't ask for any evidence.

Haiti

In fact it is easy to prove that. We don't have to make up cases. So for example, for the last several years, Haiti has been requesting the United States to extradite Emmanuel Constant. He is a major killer. He is one of the leading figures in the slaughter of maybe 4000 or 5000 people in the years in the mid 1990s, under the military junta, which incidentally was being, not so tacitly, supported by the Bush and the Clinton Administrations contrary to illusions. Anyway he is a leading killer. They have plenty of evidence. No problem about evidence. He has already been brought to trial and sentenced in Haiti and they are asking the United States to turn him over. Well, I mean do your own research. See how much discussion there has been of that. Actually Haiti renewed the request a couple of weeks ago. It wasn't even mentioned. Why should we turn over a convicted killer who was largely responsible for killing 4000 or 5000 people a couple of years ago. In fact, if we do turn him over, who knows what he would say. Maybe he'll say that he was being funded and helped by the CIA, which is probably true. We don't want to open that door. And he is not he only one.

Costa Rica

For the last about 15 years, Costa Rica which is the democratic prize, has been trying to get the United States to hand over a John Hull, a US land owner in Costa Rica, who they charge with terrorist crimes. He was using his land, they claim with good evidence, as a base for the US war against Nicaragua, which is not a controversial conclusion, remember. There are the World Court and Security Council behind it. So they have been trying to get the United States to hand him over. Hear about that one? No.

They did actually confiscate the land of another American landholder, John Hamilton. Paid compensation, offered compensation. The US refused. Turned his land over into a national park because his land was also being used as a base for the US attack against Nicaragua. Costa Rica was punished for that one. They were punished by withholding aid. We don't accept that kind of insubordination from allies. And we can go on. If you open the door to questions about extradition it leads in very unpleasant directions. So that can't be done.

Reactions in Afghanistan

What about the reactions in Afghanistan? The initial proposal, the initial rhetoric was for a massive assault which would kill many people visibly and also an attack on other countries in the region. The Bush Administration wisely backed off from that. They were being told by every foreign leader, NATO, everyone else, every specialist, I suppose, their own intelligence agencies that that would be the stupidest thing they could possibly do. It would simply be like opening recruiting offices for bin Laden all over the region. That's exactly what he wants. And it would be extremely harmful to their own interests. So they backed off that one. And they are turning to what I described earlier which is a kind of silent genocide. You can figure it out if you do the arithmetic.

A sensible proposal which is kind of on the verge of being considered, but it has been sensible all along, and it is being raised, called for by expatriate Afghans and allegedly tribal leaders internally, is for a UN initiative, which would keep the Russians and Americans out of it, totally. These are the two countries that have practically wiped the country out in the last 20 years. They should be out of it. They should provide massive reparations. But that's their only role. A UN initiative to bring together elements within Afghanistan that would try to construct something from the wreckage. It's conceivable that that could work, with plenty of support and no interference. If the US insists on running it, we might as well quit. We have a historical record on that one.

You will notice that the name of this operation. Remember that at first it was going to be a Crusade but they backed off that because public relations agents told them that that wouldn't work. And then it was going to be Infinite Justice, but the PR agents said, wait a minute, you are sounding like you are divinity. So that wouldn't work. And then it was changed to Enduring Freedom. We know what that means. But nobody has yet pointed out, fortunately, that there is an ambiguity there. To endure means to suffer. And a there are plenty of people around the world who have endured what we call freedom. Again, fortunately we have a very well-behaved educated class so nobody has yet pointed out this ambiguity. But if its done there will be another problem to deal with. But if we can back off enough so that some more or less independent agency, maybe the UN, maybe credible non-governmental organizations can take the lead in trying to reconstruct something from the wreckage, with plenty of assistance and we owe it to them. Then maybe something would come out. Beyond that, there are other problems.

An easy way to reduce the level of terror

We certainly want to reduce the level of terror, not escalate it. There is one easy way to do that and therefore it is never discussed. Namely stop participating in it. That would automatically reduce the level of terror enormously. But that you can't discuss. Well we ought to make it possible to discuss it. So that's one easy way to reduce the level of terror.

Beyond that, we should rethink the kinds of policies, and Afghanistan is not the only one, in which we organize and train terrorist armies. That has effects. We're seeing some of these effects now. September 11th is one. Rethink it.

Rethink the policies that are creating a reservoir of support. Exactly what the bankers, lawyers and so on are saying in places like Saudi Arabia. On the streets it's much more bitter, as you can imagine. That's possible. You know, those policies aren't graven in stone.

And furthermore there are opportunities. It's hard to find many rays of light in the last couple of weeks but one of them is that there is an increased openness. Lots of issues are open for discussion, even in elite circles, certainly among the general public, that were not a couple of weeks ago. That's dramatically the case. If a newspaper like *USA Today* can run a very good article, a serious article, on life in the Gaza Strip, there has been a change. The things I mentioned in the *Wall Street Journal*, that's change. And among the general public, I think there is much more openness and willingness to think about things that were under the rug and so on. These are opportunities and they should be used, at least by people who accept the goal of trying to reduce the level of violence and terror, including potential threats that are extremely severe and could make even September 11th pale into insignificance.

'Humanitarian intervention'

Harold Pinter

The playwright Harold Pinter received an honarary degree from the University of Florence. This was his acceptance speech, which was made on 10 September 2001, the day before the New York and Washington atrocities.

It will come as no surprise to you, I'm sure, when I say that how we use language has always been, for me, a major preoccupation. Recently, I have been particularly interested in the term "humanitarian intervention" as used by NATO to justify its bombing of Serbia.

I would like to read you an eyewitness account of the NATO bombing of the market place of Niš in 1999. The writer is Eve-Ann Prentice.

'The little old lady looked as if she had three eyes. On closer inspection, it was the effect of the shrapnel which had drilled into her forehead and killed her.

At first, the dead seemed almost camouflaged among the rubble, splintered trees and broken glass, but once you began to notice them, the bodies were everywhere, some covered in table cloths and blankets, others simply lying exposed where they had fallen. Houses with picket fences and window boxes bursting with blooms were now riddled with scars. Widows in black leant on their garden gates, whimpering into handkerchiefs as they surveyed their dead neighbours lying amid the broken glass, gashed trees, smouldering cars and crumpled bicycles. Plastic bags lay strewn near many of the dead, spilling parcels of fruit, eggs and vegetables, fresh from the market.

It was Friday 7th May 1999 in the southern city of Niš and NATO had, they said, made a mistake. Instead of hitting a military building near the airport about three miles away, the bombers had dropped their lethal load in a tangle of back streets close to the city centre. At least thirty-three people were killed, and scores more suffered catastrophic injuries; hands, feet and arms shredded or blown away altogether, abdomens and chests ripped open by shards of flying metal.

This had been no "ordinary" shelling, if such a thing exists. The area had been hit by cluster bombs, devices designed to cause a deadly spray of hot metal fragments when they explode.'

The bombing of Niš was no 'mistake'. General Wesley K. Clark declared, as the NATO bombing began: 'we are going to systematically and progressively attack, disrupt, degrade, devastate and ultimately – unless President Milosevic complies with the demands of the international community – destroy these forces and their facilities and support'. Milosevic's 'forces', as we know, include television stations, schools, hospitals, theatres, old people's homes – and the market place in Niš. It was, in fact, a fundamental feature of NATO policy to terrorise the civilian population.

The bombing of Niš, far from being a 'mistake' was, in fact, an act of murder. It stemmed from a 'war' which was in itself illegal, a bandit act, waged outside all recognised parameters of International Law, in defiance of the United Nations, even contravening NATO's own charter. But the actions taken, we are told, were taken in pursuance of a policy of 'humanitarian intervention', and the civilian deaths were described as 'collateral damage'.

'Humanitarian Intervention' is a completely new concept. But President George W. Bush is also following in the great American presidential tradition by referring to 'freedom-loving people' (I must say I would be fascinated to meet a 'freedom-hating people'). President Bush possesses quite a few 'freedom-loving' people himself – not only in his own Texas prisons but throughout the whole of the United States, in what can accurately be described as a vast gulag – 2 million prisoners in fact – a remarkable proportion of them black. Rape of young prisoners, both male and female, is commonplace. So is the use of weapons of torture as defined by Amnesty International – stun guns, stun belts, restraint chairs. Prison is a great industry in the United States – just behind pornography when it comes to profits.

There have been, and remain, considerable sections of mankind for whom the mere articulation of the word 'freedom' has resulted in torture and death. I'm referring to the hundreds upon hundreds of thousands of people throughout Guatemala, El Salvador, Turkey, Israel, Haiti, Brazil, Greece, Uruguay, East Timor, Nicaragua, South Korea, Argentina, Chile, the Philippines and Indonesia, for example, killed in all cases by forces inspired and subsidised by the United States. Why did they die? They died because to one degree or another they dared to question the status quo, the endless plateau of poverty, disease, degradation and oppression which is their birthright. On behalf of the dead, we must regard the breathtaking discrepancy between United States government language and United States government action with the absolute contempt it merits.

The United States has, in fact, since the end of the Second World War, pursued a brilliant, even witty, strategy. It has exercised a sustained, systematic, remorseless and quite clinical manipulation of power world-wide, while masquerading as a force for universal good. But at least now – it can be said – the US has come out of the closet. The smile is still there of course (all United States Presidents have always had wonderful smiles) but the posture is infinitely more naked and more blatant than it has ever been. The Bush Administration, as we all know, has rejected the Kyoto agreement, has refused to sign an agreement which would regulate the trade of small arms, has distanced itself from the Anti-Ballistic Missile Treaty, the Comprehensive Nuclear Test Ban Treaty and the Biological Weapons Convention. In relation to the latter, the United States made it quite clear that it would agree to the banning of biological weapons as long as there was no inspection of any biological weapons factory on American soil. The United States has also refused to ratify the proposed International Criminal Court of Justice. It is bringing into operation the American Service Members Protection Act, which will permit the authorisation of military force to free any American soldier taken into International Criminal Court custody. In other words, they really will 'send in the Marines'.

Arrogant, indifferent, contemptuous of International Law, both dismissive and manipulative of the United Nations – this is now the most dangerous power the world has ever known – the authentic 'rogue state' – but a 'rogue state' of colossal military and economic might. And Europe – especially the United Kingdom – is both compliant and complicit, or, as Cassius in Julius Caesar put it: we 'peep about to find ourselves dishonourable graves.'

There is, however, as we have seen, a profound revulsion and disgust with the manifestations of United States power and global capitalism which is growing throughout the world, and becoming a formidable force in its own right. I believe a central inspiration for this force has been the actions, and, indeed, the philosophical stance of the Zapatistas in Mexico. The Zapatistas say (as I understand): 'Do not try to define us. We define ourselves. We will not be what you want us to be. We will not accept the destiny you have chosen for us. We will not accept your terms. We will not abide by your rules. The only way you can eliminate us is to destroy us, and you cannot destroy us. We are free.'

It is certainly true that the police action in Genoa recently made it clear that the forces of reaction and repression remain savage, vicious and merciless.

But we are free. And I believe this brutal and malignant world machine must be recognised for what it is, and resisted.

Statement made to the Italian Press – 13th September 2001.

My speech at the University of Florence (10th September 2001) was highly critical of the NATO action in Serbia and other manifestations of US foreign policy. Nowhere in this speech, however, did I advocate violence. I was not throwing bombs, I was using words. The atrocities in New York and Washington are horrific, appalling. No responsible person can regard them in any other light.

United States, the West, and the rest of the world

Johan Galtung

The world will never be the same again after the terrible attack on the economic US, the military US, the foreign policy US, and on human beings like all of us. We embrace the victims of the violence, of all violence, in deep grief, and express our hope that the perpetrators will be brought to justice. Violence at this level can only be explained by a very high level of dehumanisation of the victims in the minds of the aggressors, often due to a very deep level of unresolved, basic conflict. The word 'terrorism' may describe the tactics, but like 'state terrorism' only portrays the perpetrator as evil, satanic, and does not go to the roots of the conflict.

The list of targets reads like a retaliation for the United States' use of economic power against poor countries and poor people, the United States' use of military power against defenceless people, and the United States' political power against the powerless. This calls to mind the many countries around the world where the United States has bombed or otherwise exercised its awesome power, directly or indirectly; adding 100,000 dying daily at the bottom of an economic system which is identified by many with United States economic, military and political power. Given the millions, not thousands, of victims, it has to be expected that this generates a desire for retaliation somewhere, some time.

The basic dividing line in this conflict is class, of countries and of people. It is not civilisation, although the United States sense of mission, manifest destiny, and the Islamic sense of righteousness are parts of it. Right now the confrontation is between the United States/West and parts of the Arab/Muslim world. But this may also be a fallacy of misplaced concreteness: the latter may possess more intention and more capability than other victims of the enormous United States/West violence since the Second World War. We should neither underestimate the extent of

Johan Galtung established the International Peace Research Institute in Oslo in 1959, and the Journal of Peace Research in 1964.

solidarity in the 'rest of the world', nor the solidarity of the world upper class: the West; and build solidarity with victims everywhere.

In placing the horrendous attack on the United States in the context of a cycle of retaliation there is no element of justification, no excuse, no guilt-attribution. There is only deep regret that this chain of violence and retaliation is a human fact. But it may also serve to make us break that vicious spiral.

With talk of Crusades from the United States, and of the fourth stage of jihad, Holy War, from Islamic quarters, the world may be heading for the largest violent encounter ever. The first jihad, against the Crusaders 1095-1291, lasted 196 years; the Muslims won. The second, against Israel, is undecided. The third, against communism in Afghanistan, ended with Soviet withdrawal and collapse as a factor ending the Cold War. Muslims are willing to die for their faith.

To prevent a slide into a large war with enormous, widespread suffering, the United States, everybody, should not rush to action. Hold it; deep self-reflection; dialogue; identify the conflicts, the issues; solve them; reconcile. Dialogue and global education in order to understand how others think, and to respect other cultures, rather than debate in order to defeat others with stronger arguments, can lead the way towards healing and closure.

Governments in the West, and also in the South, cannot be relied upon to do this; they are too tied to the United States, and they are also too afraid of incurring the wrath of the United States. Only people can do this, only the global civil society can. What is needed as soon as humanly possible is a massive peace movement, this time North-South. It worked last time, East-West. The future of the world is more than ever in the hands of the only source of legitimacy: people everywhere.

The unfolding design

Achin Vanaik

Beyond the common condemnation of, and horror about, the tragedies of September 11th in New York and Washington there has emerged a serious political divide in India concerning the American proposals and preparations for fighting 'international terrorism' through an international coalition of states led by itself. This is not the usual divide between Left and Right (though one can easily imagine where each would line up) but essentially between those who are morally and politically cynical and selective about defining the agents of international terrorism and therefore about fighting them, and those who insist on a moral-political universalism and impartiality. That is to say, between those who prioritise the application of uniform principles of international justice above other considerations, and those who prioritise foreign policy interests, i.e. seeking 'advantage' out of current United States policy preoccupations.

The latter talk of eliminating Islamic and other terrorist groups and of certain selected countries (like Pakistan) being terrorist states because they sponsor cross-border terrorism. But of course, state terrorism is only selectively identified. The Indian state's repressions in Kashmir or the Northeast are not considered. The government which has no remote rival in the number of civilians (in the millions) it has killed outside its own borders, or in the scale of its use of nuclear (in Japan), chemical (in Vietnam), biological (in Cuba) weapons, or in the frequency with which it has flouted international norms and rulings, is the United States. But since the Indian state and its supporting chorus which make up so much of the 'foreign policy establishment' are so keen to become strategic allies of the United States, how can it dare to accuse the US of terrorism? Besides, wouldn't it be insensitive to do so at this juncture?

In fact, this precisely is the time when the United States must be so reminded and

Achin Vanaik, together with Praful Bidwai, is the author of New Nukes: India, Pakistan and Global Nuclear Disarmament *(Signal Books, £12.99, 2000).*

criticised for its own atrocious record of terrorism; when it must be declared that the fight against terrorism must include the indictment of all states as well of sub-state agencies which are guilty. At a time when the United States along with selected allies is making itself an international anti-terrorist task force, it must be announced as widely as possible that the elementary principles of justice are flouted when agencies of terrorism, themselves unpunished and unrepentant, are not only allowed to become the judges and policemen of terrorism, but actually hailed and legitimised for playing this role. Any commitment to principles of moral and legal impartiality has to insist that the task of adjudicating on and enforcing any sentence regarding the international crime committed on September 11 must fall on an international mechanism like the International Criminal Court (whose setting up has been opposed by the United States and India) and through appropriate procedures involving an unmanipulated United Nations.

Opposing the United States effort to set up an international concert of nations behind it to justify its waging war on Afghanistan is all the more imperative because there is a much deeper design behind it all. In declaring that when it comes to retaliation there will be no distinction between the specific agency of terrorism and the country harbouring such agents, and that the USA's response to what is effectively an international crime must be a long-term war, Washington has calculatedly sought to massively extend the scope of its reaction in keeping with its much larger strategy for furthering its global aims behind the mask of 'fighting international terrorism'. It is extraordinary that so many in India have failed to understand this. The United States is demanding through its unfolding 'long term programme of 8-10 years to fight terrorism' an effective *carte blanche* to militarily-politically intervene in any country which it deems to be providing a 'safe haven' for any 'terrorists' identified as such by the US alone. Washington has also put the world on warning that it feels free to topple regimes it considers to be supporting the 'world-wide network of terrorism'. Indeed, toppling the Taliban regime establishes a vital precedent for the United State's longer term perspectives.

What the United States is doing is thus another systematic step forward in a longer game plan that has unfolded since the end of the Cold War. In 1991, quite unexpectedly, the United States found itself dominant in the system of nation states in a way that has never existed for any single country in over a century. During the first half of the twentieth century the eminence of Britain was being challenged by the United States, Germany and Japan. After the Second World War, the Soviet Union challenged the United States. After 1991, in the beginning uncertainly, later on more clearly and determinedly, the United States has gone about extending and consolidating this unique situation of its uncontested global pre-eminence on all fronts — economic, cultural, political and military. The 1991 Gulf War became the excuse for Washington to reinforce control over the Middle East and its oil. Afghanistan and Central Asia have been throughout the nineties an arena in which the United States has sought an increasing influence for itself and for its multinationals, given the oil-gas potential of the region. This has required wooing the Central Asian Republics away from Russian dominance and considering ways of expanding its influence in Afghanistan itself. Thus on three occasions the US considered recognising the Taliban regime in return for concessions concerning the building of oil and gas pipelines from Central Asia to more amenable seaboards. They have by no means lost sight of this issue of strengthening American control of energy resources in this region in this current 'war against terrorism'.

In Europe, the central issue posed after the Cold War was what would be the shape of the new security architecture? Here there were three alternatives — strengthening the European Union's/Western European Union's independent defence force or the Organisation for Co-operation and Security in Europe (OCSE) or NATO. The first two approaches would have involved the diminution of American, and the expansion of German and Russian influence in Europe. The sub-text of the Balkans conflict (Bosnia, Kosovo, Macedonia) was the emergence of the United States as the principal arbiter of European affairs. Along with the consolidation and expansion of NATO, the pre-eminence of the United States in Europe was thereby established. The ascendancy of the distinctively Anglo-American form of contemporary capitalist globalisation called neo-liberalism reflects the success of the United States in clawing back part of the economic ground lost earlier to Germany and Japan. The National Missile Defence programme represents the United States search for nuclear dominance and eventual control of space so as to establish a unilateral military supremacy over the globe. The one big US failure in the post-Cold War era was its inability to drive a wedge between the Ukraine and Russia, the two most powerful countries to emerge from the wreckage of the former Soviet Union.

The Balkans also provided precedents for American expansion through manipulation of the universal human rights discourse. And now in this 'war against terrorism', once again through a manipulation of a crucial human rights issue, the United States seeks to establish a flexibility and freedom for conventional military intervention (including the right to topple regimes) throughout the world that is truly unprecedented. And any number of countries for parochial and short-sighted gains are even prepared to be part of a coalition legitimising this effort! That the Indian Government backed by its usual set of factotums, courtiers and salespersons (i.e. the 'foreign policy establishment') is desperate to join this coalition is testimony not only to its moral hypocrisy in the fight against international terrorism but also to its incredible political naivety regarding the larger scheme of things.

Thule and Star Wars

Steve Boggan

Steve Boggan works on The Independent *in London. He filed these two stories about the impact of Star Wars on Greenland from aboard Greenpeace's MV Arctic Sunrise, Qaanaaq, Greenland in August 2001.*

I

The sign that greets arrivals at Thule airport in Greenland says: 'Air Force Space Command's 12th Space Warning Squadron. Latitude 76 degrees 32N, Longitude 68 degrees 42W.' In simple terms, this is the last place on earth you can land in a passenger jet.

As the sign says, it is the home of a United States space command squadron, a group of men and women whose job involves providing America with advance warning of airborne attack. If President George Bush gets his way, it will be one of two bases outside the US – the other is at Fylingdales, North Yorkshire – that will be key to his plans for ballistic missile defence, aka 'Son of Star Wars'.

Because of its remote location, some 800 miles north of the Arctic Circle, President Bush could be forgiven for believing this would be the less troublesome of the two foreign stations he needs permission to use if his system is to work. But he would be wrong.

This base and, more importantly, a tiny community of Inuit people evicted to make way for it, are about to find themselves at the centre of American foreign policy making. As Andy Warhol might have put it, these hunters in their 650-strong community at Qaanaaq, the northernmost municipality on the planet, are about to get their 15 minutes of fame.

Theirs is a story of enforced eviction, a nuclear plane crash, environmental pollution and national betrayal. And, after nearly 50 years of being ignored, they view President Bush's Star Wars proposals – that will see the 1972 Anti-Ballistic Missile Treaty with Russia torn up, and which China has already predicted will result in a new nuclear arms race – as their last chance to have the world sit up and take notice.

The Americans first became interested in Thule – also known as Pituffik – in 1946 when it became obvious the new threat to its interests would come from the Soviet Union. Inuit tribesmen remember the day they arrived.

'It was in April 1946,' said Aron Qaavigaq, then a 12-year-old living off the traditional Dundas mountain hunting grounds on the north-western edges of Greenland. 'We saw a plane coming out of Canada. It circled and went away. Then, in July, a huge black plane came. We saw it coming lower and lower to the sea and it landed on it, throwing out an anchor like a boat. Many people were amazed to see that. They came ashore and gave us apples and told us a ship was on its way.'

Within months, 36 ships had arrived, an airstrip was laid, and a weather station built with the permission of the Kingdom of Denmark, of which Greenland is a part. The Inuit continued to hunt for seals, walruses, whales, narwhals, foxes and birds until, between 1951 and 1953, militarisation of the base began. Finally, in May 1953, the 27 families that made up the Inuit community were told to leave to make way for American surface-to-air missile batteries. They were given between 48 hours and two weeks to get out.

Mr Qaavigaq said: 'We were told there were houses waiting for us in Qaanaaq [100 miles away], but those of us who didn't go voluntarily would not get one. We had no choice; we had to go. There were seven of us. I remember my mother and father were crying. We were young and very excited to be going somewhere new. But they kept crying, so we knew there was something wrong. Everyone packed what they could on their dogsleds and set off north across the ice. After a while, my father stopped and looked back. He and my mother were crying again.' In all, more than 150 people were forcibly evicted. And, when they arrived at Qaanaaq, the houses they were promised had not been built. For three months, they had only tents in which to live.

'They were treated appallingly,' said Christian Harlang, a Danish human rights lawyer, who has taken up their case. 'Most were given just 48 hours to leave with their elderly and their children. For decades, the Danish government lied about them, claiming they had moved voluntarily. At school, we were taught that Denmark did not mistreat Greenland the way the French and the British mistreated their colonies, yet all the time these people were suffering.'

But things were to get worse. Uusaqqak Qujaakitsoq, vice-president of the Inuit Circumpolar Conference, and Axel Lund Olsen, deputy mayor of Qaanaaq, said the new hunting-grounds were not so good. It was too far to travel back to the old grounds (and, even then, permits were required from the Danes) and, as the next generations came along, many turned their backs on the hunting way of life.

Today, unemployment in Qaanaaq is high, feelings of resentment are growing and alcoholism is becoming a serious problem. One of the reasons hunting has become so difficult, they say, is that the area has become polluted – not least because of an incident on 21 January 1968 when an American B-52 Stratofortress carrying four hydrogen bombs crashed on the ice in Bylot Sound near the Thule base. In the ensuing explosions, the bombs were fragmented, spewing radioactive debris across the snow.

Despite clean-up attempts, the Americans and Danes have admitted that between 500g and 1.8kg of plutonium – enough for a whole bomb – was never recovered. Mr Qujaakitsoq said: 'We are finding many deformed animals – musk oxen with deformed hooves and seals with no hair. We believe a lot of the pollution must be coming from the base, perhaps from the missing plutonium.'

The Danish and American governments have conducted environmental-impact studies on the base, but the results of some of them remain secret. Greenpeace, which is supporting the Qaanaaq Inuits, has tried to use Danish Freedom of Information legislation to gain access to a 4,000-page report on Thule, but to no avail. All of which makes the community fervently opposed to the Thule base being used to house the still-experimental X-band radar systems required to make President Bush's Star Wars plan a reality.

For Star Wars to work, a number of American bases plus Fylingdales and Thule would operate with X-band, which is intended to track missiles during the 'intermediate' phase of their trajectory, after launch but before their final attack phase. Other bases, including Menwith Hill in North Yorkshire, will perform a role, but it is the X-band radar bases that are the most controversial.

The Danish government, like the British, has refused to support or oppose the US proposal, arguing that the Americans have, as yet, presented no firm plans or requests for the use of bases. The Greenlandic Home Rule Government – which must defer foreign and defence issues to Denmark – has also been quiet on the issue. But in Qaanaaq, the three main local parties are all opposed to the American plans.

'People are opposed to Star Wars for two reasons,' said Mr Olsen. 'First, they are afraid that some day there will be a war and this whole area will be destroyed in a nuclear attack. Second, we are fighting for the Americans to clean up Thule and give it back to us. If the Danish government gives permission for the Americans to use it for Star Wars, we may never get our homeland back.'

The strength of feeling can be judged by the success of a Greenpeace visit to Qaanaaq. A few years ago, a ship such as the *Arctic Sunrise* would have been chased away by hunters who still bitterly remembered their trade in seal skins being affected by Greenpeace's campaign against the clubbing of harp seal pups in Newfoundland. This week, however, the *Arctic Sunrise* has been welcomed with open arms. Dan Hindsgaul, Greenpeace's disarmament campaigner, said: 'It has been a powerful experience for us to meet these people – they have been pushed around for 50 years but now they have a unique opportunity to prevent a new nuclear arms race. There are only a few of them, but they are our best chance of stopping Bush's madcap plans for Thule air base.'

Regardless of public opinion, the role of the Danish Supreme Court, which in the autumn of 2002 will rule on the Inuits' right to reclaim their old hunting-grounds, will be crucial. In August 1999, a Qaanaaq pressure group called Hingitaq 53 (Hingitaq means 'the exiled') won an historic victory in the Danish Eastern District High Court. Mr Harlang, the group's advocate, successfully argued that, under the United Nations convention on the rights of indigenous and tribal peoples – and under the Danish constitution – the people of Qaanaaq had been unlawfully moved. They were granted paltry compensation – about £1,500 each – but the victory was hugely symbolic. They have launched an appeal seeking an increase in the compensation award and will argue that it was perverse to admit they were wrongly moved without giving them the right to return.

Mr Harlang said: ‘I find it very odd that the court agreed with our argument yet did not agree to their rights to reclaim the land. I believe we have a sound case for the Supreme Court appeal and we should win it, but I don’t know if we will.

There is enormous political pressure on the court. What you have to realise is that although we are taking on the Danish government, *de facto* and *inter alia*, this is really a case between the people of Qaanaaq and the American government; the smallest, most remote population on earth against one of the most populous and the most powerful.’

Mr Qaavigaq hopes for victory but believes he will never return to his home. ‘I don’t feel bitter towards the Americans,’ he said. ‘But if Mr Bush were here now I would say, “Mr Bush, if God wanted to end the world and to turn the mountains upside down so that they were covered by the sea, he would do it; he does not need you to do it for him”.’

II

Bush’s new ‘Star Wars’ base a radioactive danger

The US Air Force base that will be twinned with Fylingdales in North Yorkshire in George Bush’s ‘Star Wars’ plans is a potential radioactive hazard with sealed missile silos containing unidentified waste and an abandoned tip where rubbish was simply pushed into the pristine waters of the Arctic.

The Independent and Greenpeace have uncovered mountains of abandoned waste and claims that workers at the Thule base in northern Greenland became ill after a B-52 crashed with four hydrogen bombs on board in 1968. There is evidence, too, of environmental pollution on a grand scale at other disused US bases in Greenland: at Marraq, where a Greenpeace team found tens of thousands of rotting barrels, and at Kulusuk on the east coast, where huge quantities of industrial scrap have been left to rust.

Thule is one of a number of forward radar bases that will be needed if President Bush’s ballistic missile defence shield is to be effective. All but Thule and Fylingdales are in territory controlled by America. To use these two bases, the United States must first obtain permission from the United Kingdom and Denmark, which governs Greenland, but opposition to the plans is mounting in both countries.

The Independent has revealed how 150 Inuit people were forcibly moved from their homes in 1953 to make way for the Thule surface-to-air missiles and how a legal challenge to reclaim their land will be heard by the Supreme Court in Denmark in autumn next year.

In the meantime, the primary concern of the Inuit, who were moved more than 100 miles (160km) north of their sacred hunting grounds on the Dundas peninsula, next to the Thule base, is that if they are given the right to return, their land will be toxic. 'I am worried that the nuclear pollution might endanger all living species,' said Vittus Qujaakitsoq, secretary to the Minister for Industry in Greenland and a prospective Social Democrat candidate for the Danish Parliament. 'We have been finding deformed animals in the area, mainly seals with no fur, and deformities of the entrails, guts and organs. These are the animals the people must hunt, so we want to know for sure whether the area is safe.'

Mr Qujaakitsoq said Greenlanders had been given assurances the area was safe after the B-52 crash, in which between 500g (1lb) and 1.8kg (4lb) of plutonium went missing in the waters of Bylot Sound, but they had been given no hard evidence. Among allegations made to *The Independent* by a number of sources are that:

- A whole H-bomb – serial number 78252 – was lost in the January 1968 crash.
- The amount of plutonium involved was higher than that admitted by the United States – up to 12kg.
- Barrels filled with contaminated ice and snow after the crash were removed to America – but some were allowed to thaw in the spring and leaked into local soil.
- Toxic sump oil was used on roads 'to keep dust levels down in summer'.

Some of the claims are impossible to evaluate because of a refusal by the United States and Danish governments to reveal details of US environmental impact reports totalling about 4,000 pages. As recently as two weeks ago, an attempt by a Greenpeace toxics campaigner, Jacob Hartmann, to gain access to a key US report, *The Thule Environmental Survey*, was rejected by the Danish Foreign Ministry, which said the US authorities were 'resisting publication'.

It is clear, however, that the Danish Environment Ministry is not happy with the American findings. On 9 June, it asked the Danish Finance Ministry for £400,000 to commission its own report, saying United States surface-to-air missile silos had been filled with waste and concreted over, and alleging that the American report had concentrated on one dump only, ignoring a second dump, landfill sites and the impact of waste on groundwater and marine life.

One former worker at the base, John Pederson, told *The Independent*: 'We used to just push waste out over the edge [into the sea]. Other workers told me they had seen radioactive waste from the B-52 crash allowed to thaw in the summer and just leak into the ground. I wanted to speak out because I am worried about the Eskimos [sic]. They eat the animals that live in the water round here.' Asked whether he had ever seen how chemicals were disposed of, he said no, but added: 'All the waste oil was put on the roads because they got very dusty in the summer.'

After the 1968 crash, some of the 1,000-plus employees who helped in the clean-up established the Thule Workers' Association when they found the incidence of cancer among their number was higher than the Danish national average. 'Mostly, the Danish workers were driving vehicles and forklift trucks containing contaminated snow, ice and equipment blown up in the crash,' said Jens Zinglersen, the association chairman. 'Today, you would see people in some kind of space suit doing that. In those days, there was no such protection, not even masks, so radioactive material was simply breathed in.'

The workers have been given small sums of compensation, but the Danish government has not admitted that the workers' illnesses – which Mr Zinglersen says includes 'strange skin cancers' – were caused by radiation. He said after the crash: 'Snow and ice was scraped up but the rest of the ice that remained there was covered in heavy carbonate sand, which sank to the bottom of the sea when the ice melted in the spring. And, in the fire, a lot of equipment melted into the ice – that all sank too.'

Mr Zinglersen said he was more critical of the Danish government than the American authorities. 'At least the Americans have provided us with thousands of pages of evidence,' he said. 'From this, we believe one bomb has never been found and is now on the bottom of the sea. They have found a bit of the casing, but not all the stages. We believe, from the evidence, that the missile was marked MK 28 and had the serial number 78252.'

In 1997, a sampling expedition conducted by a Greenland Home Rule ship, the *Adolf Jensen*, found that 'hot particles are still present after 29 years: high anomalies signifying hot particles have been identified not only in the 10-15cm [4in-6in] peak layer, but also in the upper biota-reworked sediment layer'.

When asked by *The Independent* why the Thule survey was being kept secret, Ole Samsing, head of N7, the Danish government department that represents Greenland's foreign interests, said: 'Because the owner of the report does not want it to be released by a third party.'

Asked who the 'owner' was, Mr Samsing replied: 'The US government.' He said it was considered sensitive during relations between the two governments over the return of a small part of the base – the table-top Dundas mountain and peninsula – which is symbolic to the Inuit but relatively useless in practical terms.

Mr Samsing said no surveys had been conducted by the Danish government since the Eighties. But three Greenpeace activists who broke into the base this week, Vincent Custers, Olivier Devaux and Lawrence Turk, said they saw evidence of waste, including a number of oil and chemical drums abandoned in a river.

The US Air Force said that it was unable to comment on *The Independent's* findings at short notice.

ASLEF

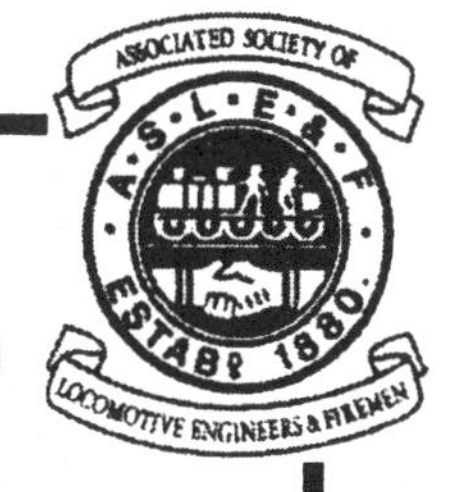

welcomes Labour's second term and calls for the following:

- **Take back the Track**
- **Government investment in Public Services**
- **No involvement in Star Wars**
- **A drive toward World Peace**
- **A charter of employment rights that would include:**

  - Equal opportunity for all and the right to work
  - Full employment
  - Employment rights from day one to prevent unfair treatment and discrimination
  - Ensure that oppressive and restrictive trade union legislation is repealed
  - Comply with the highest international conventions and standards, and
  - provide possitive laws encouraging trade union rights to represent their members individually and collectively

ASLEF also calls for all unions to support the campaign to promote public services and state pensions

M. D. RIX General Secretary ASLEF

THE BERTRAND RUSSELL PEACE FOUNDATION

PEACE DOSSIER

2001 Number 3

EUROPEAN NETWORK FOR PEACE AND HUMAN RIGHTS LAUNCH CONFERENCE

The Russell Foundation called for the renewal of the mass peace movement in Europe in the summer of 1999. As we have reported in previous issues of *The Spokesman*, the proposal received widespread support and encouragement. Since that time we have consulted extensively about these matters, including at two international consultations held in the European Parliament in Brussels and at a series of national meetings. Now we are preparing for the launch Conference of the new European Network for peace movements which takes place at the Brussels Parliament on 31 January/1February 2002*.

Of course, we live with changed circumstances after September 11th. The onslaught against the twin towers of the World Trade Centre killed thousands of innocent people. Truly, this was a massacre of the innocents. Now, President Bush has launched a massive retaliatory strike against Afghanistan. The world will be fortunate if even larger numbers of Afghans, who are also completely innocent, are not killed in these reprisals. Worse, there is evidence that this new war could spill into neighbouring territories, launching what may become a prolonged war.

From the beginning, the rational response to these horrors was to take this problem to the recognised international fora, and to seek to reach a general agreement on the necessary measures to combat terrorism. Why did the United States not do this, and launch a war instead? Why do they refuse to support the establishment of an international criminal court? How can international law prevail when each proclaims his own gun rule?

The answer to these questions is contained in the answer to another. Why have the Americans sought to jettison the treaties which have up to now, albeit inadequately, controlled the nuclear arms race? They have been bent upon removing the Anti-Ballistic Missile Treaty in order to launch what they call 'Missile Defence', but which is more commonly known as 'Son of Star Wars'. This is really an advance programme for war-fighting in and from space, which is contrary to the commitments made in the Outer Space Treaty.

Further, behind the militarisation of space lies the systematic elaboration of the American military doctrine of 'Full Spectrum Dominance'. This doctrine envisages the unchallengeable operation of United States forces 'in all domains

– space, sea, land, air and information.' And, given the global nature of US interests, it asserts that 'the United States must maintain its overseas presence forces and the ability to rapidly project power world-wide in order to achieve full spectrum dominance.'

European peace movements need to take urgent steps to link up with all those other peoples, including especially the American peoples, whose own safety is continually put at risk in this new and lethal conflict. That is why we have called a Conference to launch a new Network for Peace and Human Rights. We seek to share the experiences of all the peace movements, and to provide assistance in common and joint actions to promote nuclear disarmament and encourage peaceful relations between states and peoples.

The war on Afghanistan, the worsening situation in Palestine and Israel, Kashmir and the Caucasus, and the increasing international instability following September 11th, all threaten wider hostilities. But the peace movements are stirring. More than 300,000 marched in Perugia against the war with other large demonstrations in Naples and Turin, while 50,000 gathered in London and Berlin. Many other demonstrations against the war include those in Calcutta, Brussels, Amsterdam, Athens, Paris, Copenhagen and Stockholm. More are planned.

We need to develop links with one another in order to ensure the most rapid organisation of the opposition. Peace movements were always internationalist, but now, more than ever, we need to co-ordinate our responses with one another, and with those of the other actors in civil society.

*Information and registration forms for the launch Conference of the European Network for Peace and Human Rights are available from Russell House, Bulwell Lane, Nottingham, NG6 0BT (e-mail: elfeuro@compuserve.com) and from our web site (www.russfound.org).

ANTI-WAR MOVEMENT GROWS WORLD-WIDE

Many protests against the war on Afghanistan are taking place throughout the world. Often they receive little press coverage, although thousands of people participate.

The demonstration called by CND on Saturday, 13th October, was the largest seen in *London* for many years. Some 50,000 people walked on a glorious sunny afternoon from Hyde Park to Trafalgar Square to support the demand to 'Stop the War', and for a peaceful resolution of the conflict. Many members of the Muslim communities joined in the march. The British Government was taken aback by the size and spirit of the manifestation, although media coverage was grossly inadequate.

At the same time, more than 3,000 people responded to the call of the Scottish

Coalition for Justice not War to demonstrate in the centre of *Glasgow.* At Menwith Hill and elsewhere simultaneous demonstrations took place in support of the Global Day of Action against the Militarisation of Space.

Amsterdam saw one of the earliest demonstrations when, on 30th September, 10,000 people joined a peace rally in the medieval central square, the Dam. This was followed by a march on 20th October, when a larger number, including 170 different groups, marched for peace.

The largest manifestations of all were in *Italy.* A quarter of a million people marched from Perugia to Assisi on Sunday, 14th October, with other huge demonstrations in Naples and Turin. Earlier, 10,000 people protested in Rome.

In *Germany,* 50,000 people converged on the beautiful Gendarme Platz by the German and French Cathedrals in Berlin on Saturday, 13th October from three different parts of the city, with another 2,500 in Stuttgart. Earlier, 3,000 people joined a demo in Hamburg, and 6,000 protested in Kassel. 5,000 school students took time off to join protests as part of a pupils' initiative against the war.

5,000 people protested in *Brussels* on Sunday, 7th October, with a further demonstration on Friday, 12th October. 20,000 demonstrated outside the EU summit in *Ghent* on Friday, 19th October. In *France*, 5,000 people marched in Paris against the war on Thursday, 11th October. Protests also took place in Lille, Bayonne, Marseille, Cahors, Lyon, St. Etienne, Clermont-Ferrand, Annecy, Toulouse, Strasbourg and Brest. Committees/networks are operating in six major cities in *Denmark*. 4,000 people participated in 20 demonstrations in nine cities in the week after bombing of Afghanistan commenced on 7th October. In *Switzerland*, Berne witnessed some 10,000 people protesting against the bombing of Afghanistan. *Norway* had 1,500 people demonstrating in Oslo. In Greece, a mass rally was held in Syntagma Square, Athens on 29th September to coincide with the Washington demonstration organised by the anti-war coalition.

There have been widespread protests outside Europe against the Afghanistan war. Apart from neighbouring Pakistan, where intense anger against the bombing is felt and expressed with great passion and frequency, 20,000 demonstrated in *Jakarta*, the Indonesian capital, on 20th October. In *Calcutta*, 100,000 braved torrential downpours to take part in a peace rally over the weekend of 13/14th October, and in *Thailand*, 30,000 demonstrated against the war on 20th October. *Japan* has seen protests almost daily, with different groups holding their own demonstrations. *Australia* saw 2,000 people at a peace rally in Adelaide, with other gatherings in Melbourne and Canberra.

Useful sources:
Globalise Resistance (www.resist.org.uk) has photos from some of these demonstrations.
News and diary of activities in Britain are available at www.stopwar.org.uk. Act Now to Stop War and End Racism (ANSWER) in the United States lists hundreds of actions (see www.internationalanswer.org).

HIROSHIMA DECLARATION, 6 AUGUST 2001

A conference of local authority representatives met in Hiroshima on the 56th anniversary of its destruction. They called for the global abolition of nuclear weapons, and this year's Hiroshima Declaration celebrates that fact.

On the first August sixth of the new century, we, the citizens of Hiroshima, living witnesses to 'the century of war', hereby declare that we will do everything in our power to make the twenty-first century one of peace and humanity, free from nuclear weapons.

We believe that humanity means our willingness to listen to the voices of all sentient beings. Humanity also means nurturing children with loving care. It means valuing reconciliation in creating the human family's common future. It means rejecting violence, and reaching peaceful agreements through the power of reason and conscience. Only humanity can assure the abolition of nuclear weapons; only humanity can ensure that nuclear weapons, once eliminated, are never re-invented.

In the twenty-first century, Hiroshima intends to soar to new heights as a city of humanity. We intend to create a spiritual home for all people, a home with compassion, a source of creativity and energy for our planet's children and youth, a city offering a personal place of rest and comfort for all, young or old, male and female.

However, the calendar end to 'the century of war' has not automatically ushered in a century of peace and humanity. Our world is still darkened not only by the direct violence of local conflicts and civil wars, but also by innumerable other forms of violence, including environmental destruction, violence-promoting publications, images, and games. Now, through advanced science and technology, some are trying to extend battlefields into space.

We need our world leaders first to look at this reality humbly and unflinchingly. They must also posses a strong will to eliminate nuclear weapons, sincerity in abiding by their agreements, which are crystallisations of human wisdom, and finally, the courage required to make reconciliation and humanity top priorities.

Many *hibakusha* and their kindred spirits, feeling called upon to shoulder the fate of the entire human race, have sought the abolition of nuclear weapons and world peace with a will strong enough to cut through solid rock. For *hibakusha*, the living hell suffered fifty-six years ago remains vivid and present even today. Thus, communicating in living form to coming generations the *hibakusha's* memories, their sense of responsibility, and their unrelenting will is the most dependable first step towards survival through the twenty-first century and on to the twenty-second century, connected by a bridge of hope.

To that end, the City of Hiroshima is investing in the revitalisation of peace education, in the broadest sense of that term. We are striving, in particular, to establish Hiroshima-Nagasaki peace study courses in major universities around the world. The basic framework for such courses will be constructed from the accomplishments of the Hiroshima Peace Institute and similar institutions where academic endeavour based on unalterable fact have brought humankind closer to truth.

This week, the citizens of Hiroshima and Nagasaki are hosting the World Conference of Mayors for Peace through Inter-city Solidarity. The conference has been organised for the express purpose of abolishing nuclear weapons, and realising world peace through truth-guided solidarity among cities, the entities that will carry most prominently the torch of humanity in the twenty-first century. It is no mere fantasy to believe that in the future, member cities of this conference will lead other municipalities in expanding the circle of nuclear-free authorities until ultimately, the entire Earth becomes one solid nuclear-free zone.

Hiroshima calls on the national government of Japan to play an active role as a mediator in Asia in creating nuclear-free zones and implementing confidence-building measures. We further expect that, as a matter of national policy, Japan will initiate an effort to conclude a global treaty that prohibits nuclear weapons forever. We demand that our government properly value the contributions made by *hibakusha,* wherever they may live, which should culminate in improved relief measures that respect their rights. Finally, we demand that our national government forge the will to abolish nuclear weapons and, in accordance with the preamble of our constitution, work with Hiroshima in the effort to create a century of peace and humanity.

On this first August sixth of the twenty-first century, it is by vowing to spread the peace of this moment through the entire twenty-first century and throughout the world that we pay our sincerest respects to the souls of all the atomic bomb victims.

Tadatoshi Akiba, Mayor, The City of Hiroshima

PERUGIA APPEAL

Hundreds of thousands of people joined the March for Peace from Perugia to Assisi on Sunday 14th October. Other big demonstrations took place in Naples and Turin. The March marked the climax of the 4th Assembly of the Peoples' UN in Perugia. These extracts are taken from the Appeal made by the Assembly. The full text and related appeals are available on the web (www.krenet.it).

On Sunday the 14th of October 2001, we, the women and men of the United Nations, will march along the road that leads from Perugia to Assisi to promote the globalisation of human rights, democracy and solidarity. Today, the world has at its disposal the necessary capacity to reach this objective. But what is needed is a change of course, to reconsider first and foremost the priorities of politics and the use of resources.

We are moved by the awareness that there are no inevitable processes, that 'another world is possible', and that in order to build it, it is necessary to promote globalisation from the bottom up: a great world alliance of women and men, organisations of civilian society, community and local institutions dedicated to the refusal of every form of violence, in practice as in language, and to substituting the culture of war by a culture of peace, the culture of savage competition by that of co-operation, exclusion by acceptance, individualism by solidarity, separation by sharing, wealth creation by redistribution, and national security by communal security.

We are moved by worry for a world that seems to be going out of control, the prisoner of a painful web of tensions, crises and strident contradictions that are the cause of inexpressible human suffering. A world in which everyone talks of peace but no one does anything to prevent the outbreak of war, or to put an end to the most terrible violations of human rights, as in Palestine, Afghanistan, Sudan, Tibet or Burma. A world in which everyone talks about justice but entire peoples are condemned, like many in Africa, to hunger, thirst or illness. A world in which everyone talks about the environment but does almost nothing to stop the greenhouse effect, or the pollution and deforestation of the planet. A world in which everyone talks about liberty and democracy but which seems to be sliding towards a global authoritarianism, where the UN declaration and international law on human rights are treated by some states like the menu in a restaurant.

We are moved by worry for those millions of people without rights of citizenship: people who appear and disappear from time to time, when an inevitable tragedy occurs, people who 'exist' only if they become 'a public order problem' or an 'opportunity to cut costs' for a multinational company. We are moved by worry for a civilian society ever more under pressure from unrestrained competition, hit by an enormous growth in insecurity (be it economic, relative to a place in the workforce and income, or health, cultural, personal, collective, environmental or political issues) and by the sensation that every certainty is less certain, that we are at the end of all rules.

We are moved by worry about the globalisation process pushed by men and companies interested only in extending their power, and maximising their profits in the shortest possible period of time, without any attention to human, social and environmental costs.

After decades of world politics influenced by the economic, financial and commercial interests of the great industrial nations and the great companies, of deregulation and the law of the strongest, of privatisation, of the expansion of the market and its ideology, and of the de-legitimisation of the United Nations, the moment has arrived to redefine the priorities of the agenda of international politics and the use of resources by shifting the focus away from the interests of the few to the good of the global public.

The world needs governments and international democratic institutions determined to put a stop to the growing international disorder, and to manage the challenges of interdependence and promote the interests of the global public. The world needs governments determined to oppose and prevent war and gross violations of human rights, to eradicate poverty and guarantee to all access to the basic human rights (the right to food, to water, to health, to education, to a home, to a dignified job…), and to guarantee freedom and the practice of democratic rights, pluralism in society, freedom of enterprise and information, alongside a determination to combat racism, xenophobia, and discrimination in all their forms, to combat epidemics, face the environmental emergencies (global warming, the destruction of biodiversity, desertification…) and to safeguard natural resources for future generations, to promote equality and distributive justice in the economy and global commerce, and to encourage scientific and technological research in the direction of human development, and making it possible for all humanity to benefit from the progress reached.

Today, more than ever, we must recognise that none of these objectives, which all maintain that they share, will be reached by the free action of the market and its globalisation, for the simple reason that the market has other priorities and objectives. What is needed, therefore, is that politics, civil society, and national and international democratic institutions take the initiative.

A great responsibility is left to the governments of the richest and most powerful countries of the world that, more than any other, hold the power, resources and the means to determine, for better or for worse, the living conditions and the future of the great part of humanity.

For this reason, we the women and men of the United Nations, aware of the responsibility and the rights that we share, and coherent with the international principles of human rights and the ideals of the United Nations Charter, firmly ask our governments to take on board another priority: the promotion of a different form of globalisation: the globalisation of human rights, democracy and solidarity…To face the great challenges that we have ahead of us and to globalise human rights, it is essential to rediscover and spread an authentic culture of solidarity and sharing. No human community can survive without solidarity: not even the planetary community we are part of. But care is needed: we are not dealing with the distribution of a little of the surplus that our world produces in abundance. That which is asked for today – to save humanity from a threatening drift – is a great investment for the promotion of justice (positive peace) and for the development of international co-operation at all levels. We have the resources. For decades we have invested in arms. Today the moment has come to spend the same resources to guarantee the real security of the people, of all peoples and the planet – rather than on Star Wars!

We denounce the irresponsible behaviour, immorality and cynicism of the governments that continue to deny the United Nations the resources and means to halt the conflicts that, from Jerusalem to Kabul, Gaza to Grozny, and Diyarbakir to Khartoum, devastate our community of humanity.

We denounce the illegal behaviour, immorality and cynicism of the governments that continue to increase the international traffic in arms (the six leading exporters being four of the permanent members of the Security Council plus Germany and Italy), who increase military spending and those who are today preparing Star Wars and provoking a new world arms race. The alternative to war (outlawed by international law) and its proliferation is the creation of an efficient system of collective security, under the international authority of the United Nations, reformed and made more democratic, with an international police force and a civilian peace corps.

The demand for solidarity, justice and peace without frontiers from every part of the world demands of each of us living in the rich cities of the west, urging us to solicit our governments to change politics, but also to reconsider our model of development, and our personal and collective lifestyle, pushing us to reduce consumerism and eliminate waste and excess, to support equal trade and promote the ethical management of savings.

Globalise human rights, democracy and solidarity: this is the pressing request that comes from a multitude of women, men and local institutions all over the world. These 'men and women of the planet' ask nothing for themselves, but for all humanity. They are only the embryo of a global civil society that is growing in accordance with the values of peace and justice, human rights and non violence. They are an extraordinary resource for our common future. In their hands and ours there lies the possibility and the responsibility to change the world.

It's not enough to ask. We need to act in person. By marching towards Assisi, as Aldo Capitini did forty years ago, we are renewing above all our commitment as free women and men, as associations and responsible local organisations, because peace and justice affirm themselves in a thousand daily actions, both individual and collective. 'Everyone has a part to play'.

THE DRESDEN APPEAL

These short excerpts are from the Appeal of the Party of Democratic Socialism in Germany, which was adopted at the Second Session of the Seventh PDS Congress on 7 October, 2001.

The attacks in New York and Washington showed that no missile system, however perfect, and no outer space bristling with reconnaissance and killer satellites could have prevented the drama. New weapons systems do not bring security. They squander economic resources; they subordinate research and development to military goals. Thinking in military categories deforms intellectual and cultural life.

NATO is totally unsuitable for combating terrorism. It arose from confrontation and its self-image is unchanged. Whether it wants to or not, NATO contributes to frontlines emerging over and over again. Its new alliance strategy, including the possibility of giving itself a mandate for world-wide interventions, does not resolve any security problems. On the contrary, it creates new ones. The new Bundeswehr concept follows this strategy. One is as wrong as the other.

Heavily armed, the world will remain without peace. Disarmament gives peace a chance. One fifth of today's military spending would suffice to ensure everyone a sustained basic supply of food, drinking water, education and public health services.

We propose disarmament, preservation and extension of international arms control treaties, resurrection of the ABM treaty and the Convention on Biological Weapons and all other conventions limiting weapons and weapons technologies; prohibition of arms exports, total nuclear disarmament, complete renunciation of the military use of outer space and no new missile systems. Lasting peaceful solutions to international conflicts must be found, especially in the Near and Middle East.

A world economic order that gives a free hand to the global players of the financial, industrial and commercial worlds, that gambles away the chances of the underdeveloped countries on the stock exchange and divides the world into attractive, less attractive and unattractive zones has been obsolete for a long time. Globalisation must be socially just, democratic and civilian.

We propose that Germany and Europe work hard for a balance of interests between North and South, East and West, poor and rich; for redistribution and international co-operation. This involves regulating the finance markets, combating poverty, promoting social development and the development of civil society, giving the economy a new ecological direction. The action programmes of numerous United Nations World Conferences have outlined how this can be done. The Kyoto Protocol is one. All these agreements must finally be implemented. It is important that people come together in resolving concrete problems, in networks, in individual projects and in an intercultural dialogue.

Since the end of the East-West conflict the USA as the sole remaining world power has used NATO as a military instrument of its global interests policy. But this has not even benefited its own security, to say nothing of European security.

The burden of preserving peace and international security should be shouldered by the entire community of nations. Internationally, security policy is the province of the United Nations alone. As long as the US administrations do not share responsibility and as long as they condemn their country to unilateral world dominance, the United States will remain, more than others, the target of global terrorism. PDS policy wants to prevent this.

Thinking in cold war categories under the motto that my enemy's enemy is my friend has to be put an end to once and for all. The PDS struggles to have the top priority of the United Nations Charter, outlawing war and the threat or use of military power, finally respected by all states in their international relations.

The United Nations and its subsidiary organisations can ensure world peace, reduce threats to individual states and set universally valid standards for a world-wide domestic policy. It must be restored to its role as the sole legitimate world organisation; it must be strengthened and at the same time reformed.

In order to survive, humanity requires recognised rules of co-operation in this one world. The Charter of the United Nations is the basis for human co-existence. This applies to Afghanistan just as it does to Macedonia and Kosovo.

All measures must be compatible with international law and the United Nations Charter. It must be implemented at last.

Terrorism must be combated internationally without respect of persons and their motives, regardless of which countries might be involved or which state interests might be affected.

Modern societies have banned retaliation and revenge from social relations; self-defence and assistance in case of need are subject to strict legal restrictions. This should also apply to preventive or repressive measures against terrorism. In a civil society, these are court and police measures, but never military strikes and war.

The Appeal ends: Mankind today has all it takes to eliminate wars, poverty and underdevelopment permanently. But mankind also has all it takes to wipe human life off the face of the earth once and for all. The looming war can still be the last throes of a millennium of violence and counter-violence. The present can still be stronger than the powers of the past. All it takes is peace!

CHOMSKY ON VANUNU

'The kidnapping of Mordechai Vanunu by the government of Israel, the farcical trial, his imprisonment for 15 years, and the savage and sadistic punishment he has been forced to endure rank high among the current crimes of states that claim to recognise human rights and democratic principle. The tolerance of these crimes by Israel's sponsors and allies is a continuing disgrace, for which they should be called to account by their citizens.

Vanunu merits enormous respect for his courage and integrity in revealing to the world what those who wished to know already knew, if not in detail, then in essentials: that with Western complicity, Israel had developed a substantial nuclear capacity, alone in the region. The nature and severity of the threat posed by these programmes is underscored by General Lee Butler, Commander-in-Chief of the US Strategic Command in the early 1990s, under the Bush and Clinton Administrations. "It is dangerous in the extreme", he warned, "that in the cauldron of animosities that we call the Middle East, one nation has armed itself, ostensibly, with stockpiles of nuclear weapons, perhaps numbering in the hundreds, and that inspires other nations to do so". It takes little imagination to spell out the likely consequences, or to recognise what they portend at the moment when this "cauldron of animosities" is on the verge of boiling over once again.

To free Mordechai Vanunu from the criminal torture to which he has been subjected is surely within the power of the United States and its allies. It is just as surely within the power of an aroused public to demand that there be no further delay in bringing this shameful episode to an end, so that those committed to peace and justice can welcome Vanunu and honour him for his contribution to the cause he has served so well, and to dedicate themselves with renewed vigour to carrying it forward, inspired by his example'.

COMMUNICATIONS

from Vassilis Dedotis

On April 6th, 2001, the Greek Parliament voted in favour of an important amendment to the Constitution: a provision allowing for civilian service and also conscientious objection.

This was a great step forward after some fifty years of persecution and harassment for those opposed to military service. Conscience objectors, almost exclusively Jehovah's Witnesses in Greece, first made their appearance here in the late 1940s. Since then, two people have been executed, five were tortured to death, 26 were sentenced to life imprisonment, 42 were sentenced to death, 68 were exiled, and over 3,000 served time in prison ranging from months to 14 years.

Personally, I served almost nine years in prison as a conscientious objector, and spent many years since working for better conditions in this regard. Although a law was enacted in 1998 providing for a civilian service, the recent amendment renders conscientious objection an indisputable constitutional right. Furthermore, legislation passed just a few weeks ago now allows for the criminal records of older conscientious objectors to be cleared. For this reason, I would like to take this opportunity to thank you and many others for all your efforts and endeavours over the years, all of which have contributed to this fine outcome. They have certainly been appreciated, and have finally borne good fruit. It is hoped that the use of conscientious objectors in constructive forms of civilian service will prove to be a boon to Greek society.

from the poet John Kinsella

Recently, I've had to do a lot of travel between America, Europe, and Australia. Every time I enter a new country, I'm made aware of the anxieties of quarantine efficiency. With foot and mouth still prevalent in Britain – despite the propaganda from the Blair Government – and present also in Europe, there is a stronger than usual vigilance at American and Australian airports. It's the same atmosphere as when the early outbreaks of Creutzfeld-Jacob disease were discovered.

Quarantine isn't just about keeping diseases out, protecting a specific geography from physical contamination, but also about the preservation of 'home' values. It is about a mental and spiritual 'purity'. For Australia, it's another form of the 'White Australia Policy', and extends from microbes to people and ideas. Information might be available via the net, media, or books, but that's quite different from allowing physical presence. Of course, the risk of remaining 'open' is that genuinely destructive forces may enter – but how often are these forces in actuality engendered from the inside, rather than originating in the feared 'outsider'.

It is worth considering the cultural politics of 'plague' diseases in farm animals. 'Mad cow' disease and 'foot and mouth' not only threaten the potential destruction of Australian rural industries, but Australian's self-image, its 'way of life'. These are diseases of an old world order, of a corruption and decay that Australia feels it might keep out.

Australia, as a nation, is itself a corruption of quarantine. It is the construct of intrusion and pollution: colonisation. In the same way that many non-indigenous Australians still refuse to accept collective and 'historic' responsibility for offences against indigenous peoples, so, too, do they work overtime on preventing 'offence' against the sanctity of their living conditions, of their spatial and metaphysical security.

The brutal incarceration of 'boat people' is a case in point. The fear is manifold: the risk of bringing 'exotic diseases' into Australia is only a peripheral one. The treatment of people as polluted herd animals is strikingly obvious if you've been outside the country for a while. They do it in the United States as well, and in Britain. It becomes an issue of power and protecting privilege. That's what quarantine is.

The contradiction inherent in this war against existing diseases is absurd. The Australian government, for example, will allow trials of genetically modified grains, and fight to keep out foot and mouth. Even outside the ethical questions regarding the interference of the structure of a living organism, doubts about safety should mean that no risks are taken. If our health is affected by GM foods, the weakened body becomes the potential host for new viruses, new mutations.

When first thinking about this letter, I'd just got back from driving out to look around the historical town of Saffron Walden in Essex, which proved as much as anything else a tour of both government and private test sites for GM crops and other kinds of genetic experimentation. Not far out of Cambridge, the Wellcome Trust has established a large facility which was heavily featured in local papers because of attempted expansion, opposed by ordinary residents. As with most such problems, the Government publicly supported only limited expansion, while in real terms overturning obstacles in order to maximise that expansion. This seems typical of the whole Government approach to biotechnology, mooted as an area with potentially great profits which Britain cannot 'afford' to miss out on. The Government then will sidestep public protest in order to secure long-term financial benefits. The experimental data that might contradict apparent benefits of particular biotechnologies are either suppressed or ridiculed.

Logically, we can choose not to alter the biology of an organism, in the same way that we can choose not to eat animals or use animal products, certainly given most social and cultural conditions. One may be alienated or ostracised by one's cultural group, which at times I, as a vegan, certainly have been. But the choice is there. Of course, some environments shape the conditions of choice in a way that excludes such options, and I respect and accept that.

However, in the case of GM it is different – education, class, wealth, and cultural priority favour those making the choices. Scientists and politicians control the flow of information, and are themselves controlled by governments, bureaucracies, and corporations. The most altruistic scientist works within a regime established for purposes of profit or nationalism, or of shaping humanity in a particular image, to a particular agenda. We all take our own prejudices to acts affecting others, especially regarding decisions about what's for the common good.

Like it or not, I am a coloniser, an oppressor, a parasite, a deceiver, and an aggressor, just like the rest of humanity. But transgenics, genetically modified organisms, introducing a jellyfish gene into a monkey making its fingernails glow, are ludicrous. Life and matter are reduced to concepts of energy – the food simulators on *Star Trek* get people excited. Fantasy blurs with reality, it takes away the need for ethical decisions. Apparently. The use of animal parts with human compatibility to lengthen lifespans in one laboratory, ways of feeding the planet's increasing population in another. The equation cancels itself out. The different hands of science work independently, then create ethics committees seemingly to homogenise their response and disorder. Thoreau wrote: 'The mass of men serve the state thus, not as men mainly, but as machines, with their bodies'. And thus we are as consumers of these lies.

from Dr Andreas Toupadakis

These excerpts are taken from an open letter which sets out the reasons for Dr Toupadakis's resignation from the Lawrence Livermore National Laboratory in the United States. The full text is available on the web (www.globalcomment.com).

This letter is an appeal to every secretary, technician, scientist, engineer, and any other person whose participation supports the world war machine to withhold their skills from weapons work and from activities that support or enable weapons work.

We have a moral obligation and duty to think, speak, and act first as citizens for a peaceful world, and next as scientists. The higher our education is, the higher our responsibilities are for a humane world. Should we talk about science before we even think about what our science is for? That is precisely what we are doing. And that is why I resigned from my position as a scientist in the nuclear weapons programme at the Lawrence Livermore National Laboratory as of January 31, 2000.

My purpose in writing this letter is to make known the reason for my resignation from the Lawrence Livermore National Laboratory. It is simply that my conscience does not allow me to work for the development or maintenance of nuclear weapons. When I was hired by Lawrence Livermore, I was not adequately informed about the specifics of my job responsibilities. After being hired, I found myself expected to work on weapons maintenance in the Stockpile Stewardship Programme. I believe that I am not alone in having this experience of not being directly informed.

If many scientists knew that sooner or later they would find themselves entangled in nuclear weapons work, would they have joined the National Laboratories? I believe that, in not levelling with people, serious questions are raised regarding the integrity of our leaders. Upon realizing on the one hand the obviously questionable practices in the workplace, and on the other hand, the real mission of the national scientific laboratories, I decided to withhold my scientific skills and resign. I cannot forget what my ancient Greek teachers taught me, which I now see being practised worldwide: "*Science without virtue is immoral science.*" – Plato

How can we continue to go back home after work every day and look in our children's eyes and tell them that we are working for a safer world for them? Have our hearts become stones? We have tried to justify our involvement in building and maintaining nuclear arsenals by claiming that we are doing it for peace. How can we have peace when, by our work on weapons, we are raising fear in the hearts of those who do not have the same technology for killing?

True peace is based on mutual trust. The argument that I have heard so many times from weapons scientists is this: since the last big war, we have not had another one, so the invention of terrible weapons of destruction has put an end to war because everyone knows how terrible it would be if they dared to start one. This is an error. Who has led them to this amazing delusion? Who has led them to lose themselves in the temporary daily demands of their scientific careers and to forget about the eternal demands of their conscience?

My fellow scientists and engineers, the national laboratories must change from labs of war to labs of peace, if there is to be a chance to avoid the extinction of all life on earth. Does non-proliferation work advance the goal of non-proliferation when, at the same time, we are building more weapons? Who are we trying to fool? Many scientists are hired at the national labs to do environmental or other work, seemingly not directly related to weapons work.

Those who work on environmental projects or non-proliferation projects at the nuclear weapons labs have not realised that such a thing is an illusion. What environmental work? What non-proliferation work? Last October 13, the US Senate voted down the 40-years-in-the-making Comprehensive Test Ban Treaty. Now, through the deceptively-named "Stockpile Stewardship" programme, not only are weapons expected to be tested, but new weapons are also to be made. In simple words: we are burying the waste so we can make more, and building more weapons so that other nations will follow our example.

We can not ignore these facts and go on with our science. Science, which ought always to be aiming at the good of humanity, is assisting in the work of destruction, and is constantly inventing new means for killing the greatest number of people in the shortest amount of time. Science that is used to terrorize people, kill them, or make them invalids is immoral science. It must be abolished immediately. Those who participate in acts of violence against humanity by using, making, or servicing weapons in the name of human rights or under any other name, in every nation of our world, must remove themselves from their jobs today. If we do not act now, we may very well see our own children become victims in ways we have never dreamed of and never expected.

The contradiction between what we love to do and what we are forced to do by our fears has brought us into a state of despair. When we make our work the centrepiece of our existence, then we will find happiness.

I know without any doubt in my heart that the people who work on nuclear weapons are as good as people who work anywhere else. I have met some people with such beautiful souls that I find it impossible to explain why they would work on weapons. They are working on science in a detached way, not thinking about what will happen as a result, outside of the laboratory.

Recently, Einstein was chosen as *Time* magazine's "Man of the Century." Most articles describe only his contribution to the discovery of nuclear energy; however, they fail to even mention that he was a strong advocate of anti-war movements, a peace activist. I wonder how many scientists have ever read the Russell-Einstein Manifesto?

'*We appeal, as human beings, to human beings: Remember your humanity and forget the rest. If you can do so, the way lies open to a new paradise; if you cannot, there lies before you the risk of universal death.*'

We urgently need an international campaign to help scientists and engineers see that they must withhold their skills from war-science. I hope that my letter of appeal will start this campaign and that individuals from every nation will offer their support for the idea. My letter is a wake-up call to all those who can hear the call of their conscience.

Having contemplated these matters, and having recognised the real and misrepresented mission of the United States National Laboratories, I have decided to resign. I cannot live my life in a way that goes against my conscience.

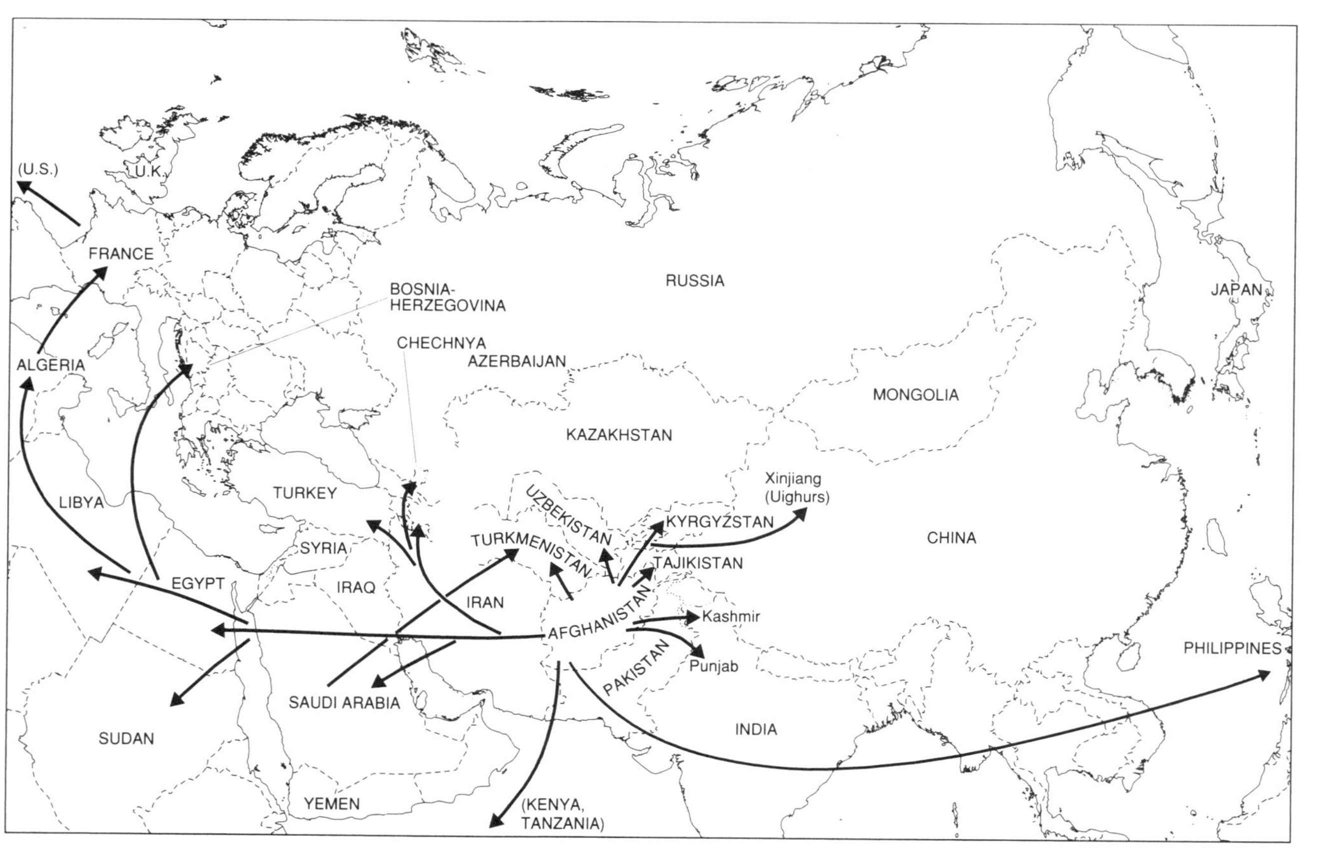

Map 2 Movements of CIA-trained guerrillas and drugs outwards from Afghanistan after the 1979–89 Afghanistan war.

Reviews

The Great Game

Michael Griffin, *Reaping the Whirlwind: The Taliban Movement in Afghanistan*, Pluto Press, pp.284, 2001, £19.99, ISBN 0745312748
John K. Cooley, *Unholy Wars: Afghanistan, America and International Terrorism*, Pluto Press pp. 300, 1999, new edition 2000, reprinted 2001, £13.99, ISBN 0745316913

Pluto Press has pulled off a small coup in publishing two books on Afghanistan within a month of the attack on New York, one a new work and the other a new edition. They are full of information that we need to have to understand the background to the events of September 11, 2001 and to have some idea of what may follow the war which the United States, with British support, has launched against the suspected perpetrators of that terrible destruction of innocent civilians. Readers of these books will no longer be so sure of the innocence of those who are now engaged on this war and who are waging the war through forming alliances especially among governments of states with Muslim populations. If such readers had not picked up some of the information in these books already, they will be amazed at the facts that are revealed with detailed reference to sources and documentation. They will not be surprised to find that the poor people of Afghanistan are once again the main sufferers from Great Power rivalries.

Afghanistan was a state maintained by the British Empire in the 19th Century as a buffer to protect the North West Frontier of India from Russian pressure on the north. This was 'The Great Game' that you can read about in Kipling's book *Kim*. It was the object of several Afghan wars and humiliating defeats for British forces followed by punitive expeditions. It has a further strategic importance as it contains the Hindu Kush, the only passage over the Himalayas from Central Asia into the Chinese province of Sinkiang, along the historic silk route. The population is a mixture of what the British called 'Pathans' and people of Persian, Turkish, Uzbek, Tajik, and other central Asian origins, as it has borders in the north with Iran, Turkmenistan, Uzbekistan and Tajikistan, as well as with Pakistan to the south. It is of crucial importance to an understanding of Afghanistan's importance in the 'Great Game', as it is now being played, to recognise the ambitions of the Central Asian states that were once part of the Soviet Union, as well as of Kazakhstan and Kyrgyzstan, which lie just beyond them to the north. When the Soviet Union broke up, they all became separate states, but Russia has tried to keep them under some sort of control through the Commonwealth of Independent States (CIS) and the deployment of Russian arms.

The Central Asian Oil States

These Central Asian states are not large in population, not much more than 40 million in total, mainly in Turkmenistan and Uzbekistan, compared with

Afghanistan's 20 million. But they are of very great economic importance. They were developed by the Soviet Union as a major source of oil, natural gas, hydro-electricity, cotton, and other agricultural products. Railways and roads were built including the Turksib line, the subject of Victor Turin's famous film. Unlike the British in Africa, the Russians made a serious effort to educate the people, to give land to the peasants and to bring them into participation in the process of development. Leonard Barnes, an English socialist, wrote a book in the 1940s entitled *Soviet Light on the Colonies*, which described these differences.

The several republics which emerged from the break-up of the Soviet Union had minority Russian populations and were educated in Russian. The Russian proportion, largest in Kazakhstan, is now dwindling as a result of lower birth rates. Under Soviet rule the populations still held on to their native language, which in all cases except for the Tajiks was Turkish, and many retained their Muslim beliefs. Indeed their new leaders, often from the old Communist élites, have rather emphasised this tradition. There has been talk about this Eurasian Balkans forming a combined Turkestan. Uzbekistan has taken the lead in this direction, and is today giving most support to the United States alliance, hoping for future favours. But despite Uzbek ambitions, internal differences – each country has mixed populations – have prevented this; and Russia has done all in its power to encourage the differences. The importance to Russia of keeping control in this area is that along with Azerbaijan on the other side of the Caspian Sea, Kazakhstan and Turkmenistan are according to *Jane's Intelligence Review* of February 1996, quoted by Michael Griffin, 'sitting on the largest known reserves of unexploited fuel in the planet'. Russia wants to ensure that this oil and gas is piped through Russia under Russian control.

The United States has other ideas for the Caspian oil. One is to take the oil across Georgia and Turkey to the Mediterranean port of Ceyhan, but this depends upon securing sufficient political stability in Georgia. Another idea was to traverse Afghanistan from Turkmenistan, to outlets in Pakistan and the Indian Ocean. In October 1995 an accord was reached in Ashkhabad, so Michael Griffin asserts, between the Turkmen Government and a joint US-Saudi venture to build a $2 billion gas pipeline across Afghanistan to Pakistan. This was the very moment when the Taliban were laying siege to Kabul, the capital of Afghanistan.

In 1997, according to Arundhati Roy (see 'War is Peace'), a delegation from the Taliban went to Houston, USA to meet US State Department officials and the oil companies. As Roy comments, nobody at the top then objected to the Taliban's crimes against humanity; only outraged American feminists complained to the President, and the deal was scuttled when the American embassies in Kenya and Tanzania were bombed. The oil companies will be trying again now.

The US Plans for Eurasia

The pipeline venture was not the first time the USA had taken an interest in Afghanistan. In 1979 Soviet armies invaded Afghanistan to support a friendly government there in fear of it being toppled by one friendly to the US. That this was a real fear was confirmed by Robert Gates, former director of the CIA, who revealed in his Memoirs *From the Shadows* that American intelligence services had begun secretly to aid the mujahadin (Islamic fighters) in Afghanistan six months before the Soviet invasion. The Soviet armies fought the Afghans for ten long years, destroyed much property, lost many thousands of lives and had to be withdrawn by Gorbachev in 1989 without having achieved their aim. At the beginning of this war Zbigniew Brzezinski was US President Carter's National Security Adviser. When Brzezinski was asked by a French journalist in 1998 whether he had provoked the Russian intervention, Michael Griffin quotes Brzezinski's reply (from *Nouvel Observateur*, Jan 15-21, 1998, p.76):

> 'It isn't quite that. We didn't push the Russians to intervene, but we knowingly increased the possibility that they would. The secret operation was an excellent idea… I wrote to President Carter 'We now have the opportunity of giving the USSR its Viet Nam war'. Indeed for almost ten years Moscow had to carry on a war unsupportable by the government, a conflict that brought about the demoralisation and finally the break-up of the Soviet Empire.'

When asked further whether he regretted having supported the Islamic fundamentalists, having given arms and advice to future terrorists, Brzezinski replied:

> 'What is more important to the history of the world? The Taliban or the collapse of the Soviet Empire? Some stirred up Muslims or the liberation of Central Europe and the end of the Cold War?'

In 1998, Brzezinski did not regard Islamic fundamentalism as a world menace. 'What is there in common,' he asked, 'among Saudi Arabian fundamentalism, moderate Morocco, Pakistan militarism, Egyptian pro-Western or Central Asian secularism? Nothing more than what unites the Christian countries.' He may have been right then, but in 2001? He wasn't taking chances, any way. A year before, he had written his book *The Grand Chessboard: American Primacy and its Geostrategic Imperatives*. This can be seen in relation to the American military plans which President Bush has espoused for establishing United States 'Full Spectrum Dominance'. In the book Brzezinski not only made clear the United States interest in bringing the Ukraine into association with NATO and away from Moscow's influence since 'Ukraine supports Georgia's efforts to become the route for Azeri [Caspian] oil exports' to the Black Sea, but, even more importantly, staked the US claim to dominance in post-Soviet Eurasia:

> 'The United States [is] … clearly interested not only in developing the region's resources, but also in preventing Russia from exclusively dominating the region's geopolitical space. In so doing, America is not only pursuing its larger Eurasian geostrategic goals but is also representing its own growing economic interest, as well as that of Europe and the Far East, in gaining unlimited access to this hitherto closed area.'

In 1979, Brzezinski's strategy for excluding the Russians still looked extremely hazardous. The only hope of defeating the Russians in Afghanistan was the financing, arming and training of mujahadin to fight a guerrilla war against the Soviets in the mountains of Afghanistan. But such a holy war, a jihad, required outside support in Muslim countries. The staunch ally of the USA, the Shah of Iran, had been overthrown early in 1979 and by the end of the year 50 US diplomats were held as hostages in the American Embassy in Teheran by revolutionary Islamic fundamentalists. How were others to be won for an American inspired anti-Soviet crusade in Afghanistan? John Cooley, who was reporting for the *Christian Science Monitor* in Washington, describes in his book how Brzezinski was sent by President Carter first to Egypt and then to Pakistan, and Defence Secretary Harold Brown to China, another potential ally.

Why to Egypt? In March of this same year, 1979, President Anwar al-Sadat of Egypt had signed a peace treaty in the Israel-Palestine conflict with US President Carter and Prime Minister Menahem Begin of Israel. For not requiring Israeli evacuation of the West Bank, Gaza and Arab East Jerusalem the treaty was denounced by most of the Muslim world. To cover his back, Sadat saw the chance of continuing his flirtation with the Islamist leaders in Egypt, which he had begun with the aim of fighting off Communist influence. What better than to involve them in helping the Americans with equipping and supplying volunteers for the Afghan jihad? The ancient Russian arms which Egypt had were sent off to be used against the Russian armies in Afghanistan, and brand new American equipment arrived in Egypt to keep Sadat in place. It failed to do that. Sadat was murdered in 1981, but Egyptians including Sheikh Omar Abdel Rahman, the moving force in the first bombing of the New York World Trade Centre, became key players in international terrorist plots, being orchestrated against the Russians by the CIA.

From Cairo John Cooley describes how Brzezinski went on to Pakistan. Why Pakistan? In that same fateful year of 1979, General Zia al-Haq had seized power in Pakistan and hanged his left-leaning predecessor Zulficar Ali Bhutto. Zia al Haq had been helped to power by extreme Muslim groups as well as by the army and was easily persuaded to give support to an Afghan jihad. Zia was particularly anxious to fend off US obstruction of Pakistan's plans to follow India in nuclear weapon development. Help for Afghan resistance had, however, to be conducted in secret through the Pakistan military intelligence institution (ISI) working closely with the CIA. This was not the first time that the 'Great Game' in Afghan affairs had been conducted through the intelligence services. It was through them that Anglo-Russian rivalry was conducted in the Nineteenth Century, as becomes clear in the last pages of Kipling's story of *Kim*.

How effective this secrecy was in the 1980s can be seen from the facts, hardly known at all at the time, which John Cooley reveals of Chinese arms supplied for use in Afghanistan against the Russians and also of British involvement in training mercenaries. Only Enoch Powell protested in the House of Commons at Mrs Thatcher's 'slavish' willingness to follow the lead of President Reagan in Afghanistan and elsewhere (quoted by Cooley from Stephen Dorril, *The Silent*

Conspiracy: Inside the Intelligence Services in the 1980s, Heinemann 1994, pp. 382-91). The 'elsewhere' may on this occasion have referred to arms deals with Saudis in which American and British firms, including Mrs Thatcher's own son, seem to have been involved.

As the Afghan jihad rolled on, more modern arms than Russian cast-offs were needed to defeat the Soviet invaders and these required money, whether they were bought from the international arms dealers or corruptly obtained from the Soviet troops themselves. Saudi Arabia could be relied upon to help, but increasingly sums became available through the drug trade. Poppies for heroin manufacture have for long been grown in Afghanistan and Pakistan (the Golden Crescent) and Central Asia has been at the centre of drug trafficking, but John Cooley provides 'overhelming evidence to show that the Afghanistan war, in which all sides used drugs as an actual weapon and as a source of finance, gave this monstrous and lucrative international business a decisive push forward' to an amount from this source estimated at 500 tons of pure white heroin, valued on New York streets at about $50 billion. Cooley reveals at the same time the exemption that was requested and granted from the US Drugs Enforcement Administration to the CIA to allow it not to have to report drug smuggling that came to its notice.

Enter Usama bin Laden

Among the many thousands of young men who responded to the call to join the jihad against the Godless Soviets was one Usama bin Laden. His family came from Yemen but had made their money in construction work in Saudi Arabia, building palaces for the house of Saud in Riyadh. By the 1970s the bin Laden conglomerate was the biggest private contractor of its kind in the world attracting engineering talent from all over and being run by young Usama. When interviewed in 1993 by Robert Fisk of *The Independent* newspaper, bin Ladin said of the Soviet invasion, 'I was enraged and went there at once'. With his wealth and background, Cooley comments that 'he seemed to Saudi intelligence and the CIA an ideal choice for the leading role he began to play... bin Laden began to pay with his own and company funds, for recruitment, transportation and training of the Arab volunteers who flocked first to Peshawar and then to Afghanistan, to fight in the jihad. According to Egyptian intelligence his aid went to the Islamist groups in Egypt, including ....the killers of Sadat....By 1985 he had collected enough millions from his family and company and from wealthy Arab Gulf merchant families, to organise al-Quaida, the Islamic Salvation Foundation, to support the jihad.' Many of those whom bin Laden recruited, Cooley comments, turned out to be zealous Muslims and brave fighters, but some were criminals engaged in money counterfeiting and laundering and in drug trafficking, activities which continued after the Russians withdrew from Afghanistan

The US State Department Fact Sheet, released in the summer of 1997, says nothing of bin Laden's CIA connections, but gives much detail of his subsequent activities as a master of Islamic and anti-American terrorism, upon which much of Mr Blair's so-called 'evidence' against bin Laden as the perpetrator of the New York

New York attacks was based. How did it come about that he switched so completely from working with the Americans to fighting against them? When the Russians withdrew from Afghanistan, the CIA trained guerrillas moved out all over the world. Cooley prints a map at the front of his book which is reproduced here on page 78 with the author's own subscript. This reads: *Movements of CIA-trained guerrillas and drugs outwards from Afghanistan after the 1979-89 Afghanistan war*. Two thousand veterans went to Algeria in 1992, according to Cooley, while other contingents surfaced in Kashmir, Somalia, Yemen, Azerbaijan, Bosnia-Hercegovina, Chechnya, Tajikistan and even the Philippines. Kosovo could be added to that list. Always the mix was 'guerrillas and drugs' and most of these places had movements which were anti-Soviet or anti-Russian. In 1990, however, bin Laden turned on his American masters.

Why? The reason for this about face was the Gulf War, not just the attack on Saddam Hussein, whom the Americans had previously supported in Iraq's war with Iran, but the establishment of an American military base in Saudi Arabia, the Islamic holy land, which bin Laden believed the Saudi ruling family should never have allowed. The Saudis were also persuaded at the same time to suspend their support for the Arab 'Afghan' cause. As Michael Griffin puts it, bin Laden 'went rogue, setting up a private base near Jalalabad and activating links with Saudi exiles in Iran and Syria. By 1994, the Saudis froze his assets and cancelled his passport, effectively declaring him a public enemy.' Two years later he was in the Sudan, where he stayed for two years rebuilding his private fortune. By 1997, he was back in Afghanistan where he was interviewed by Robert Fisk of *The Independent* and Peter Arnett of CNN, to whom he made his declaration of jihad against US soldiers in Saudi Arabia.

From here on the question has to be asked, according to Michael Griffin, 'Was he the Taliban's honoured guest or a hostage?' It seems that in 1998 he moved from his armoured cave north of Jalalabad to a house near Kandahar, but early in 1999 he vanished with his family and close followers, heavily armed, somewhere it was thought into the mountains in the north. By then he was wanted for 'inciting' the bombing of the US embassies in Nairobi and Dar es Salaam. For this President Clinton ordered reprisal bombings on a Sudanese pharmaceutical company and on camps in Afghanistan where some of bin Ladin's supposed trainees were killed, but not bin Ladin.

Who are the Taliban?

After the Soviet withdrawal from Afghanistan, in 1989, bitter battles broke out between armed rival ethnic and religious groups, some 170 of them that had just managed to stay together against the common Soviet enemy. Anyone who proposes today replacing the Taliban with a united alternative government 'when' the Taliban are defeated should read Cooley's and Griffin's descriptions of the years between 1989 and 1996. Some towns and cities were captured and recaptured several times leaving more ruined buildings than even the Russians had destroyed. Then, in 1994, Kandahar fell to an obscure militia of religious immediately called for 4000 volunteers from Pakistan. It is widely supposed that the Taliban had the support of key figures in the army and secret service in Pakistan as well as in Pakistan's fundamentalist Islamic groups, and possibly of the CIA in view of its close ties with the Pakistan intelligence services. In the next year the Taliban laid siege to Kabul but failed to capture the capital until September of 1996. Afghanistan was then declared a 'completely Islamic state' under the leadership of Mohammad Omar. Women were denied education and forced to cover their faces. In May 1997, Pakistan recognised the Taliban government, followed by Saudi Arabia and the United Arab Emirates.

It was, therefore, from Taliban controlled Afghanistan in February 1998 that Usama bin Ladin called on Muslims to 'kill the Americans and their allies – civilian and military' – and brought down upon that unhappy country the cruise missiles aimed by the US Navy at bin Ladin's camps. Saudi Arabia once more withdrew its diplomats and the UN deferred decision on recognition. But Pakistan maintained its support, the new military dictator, General Musharraf, having been put in power in October 1999, as it appears from Michael Griffin's account, by the most fundamentalist Islamic groups in the country, which are strong Taliban supporters. The occasion for his taking power was opposition to action taken by Pakistan generals to close down the terrorist camps in Afghanistan. This time they were against the terrorists because, of course, they were now no longer killing Russians but Americans. Pakistani opinion was divided. The Taliban were their brothers but the country owed huge debts to America. No wonder it is proving difficult to bring Musharraf on side with the Bush-Blair alliance against the Taliban. Between the New York attack and the reprisals against Afghanistan it was possible to separate Pakistan from the Taliban, but for how long now?

What to do?

What both these books show with frightening clarity is the depth of the involvement of the American intelligence services, the CIA, in recruiting, training and deploying international terrorist groups like those of bin Ladin in their 'Great Game' against the control of the Soviet/Russian empire over Central Asia. This is seen to explain the extension of American arms and forces into Palestine, into Cyprus, into Somalia, into Bosnia, into Kosovo, into Saudi Arabia, into the Ukraine and now into Uzbekistan and Afghanistan itself. It is not necessary to accept the wilder stories of some American commentators who see the hand of the CIA even in the bombing of New York, with the aim of establishing the right to occupy Afghanistan, for one to have doubts about the CIA's total failure to anticipate that terrible revenge by the United States Government's own creatures upon Americans themselves. The title of Michael Griffin's book is *Reaping the Whirlwind*, and it was written before the horror of September 11, when the whirlwind destroyed 6000 innocent people. But how many had been killed before them from the machinations of the CIA?

These books were written before the bombing of New York, and the authors were, even before that terrible event, anxious about the response of Muslim Arab opinion to American eastward expansion. They must be even more anxious today as Bush and Blair pursue their 'crusading war' against a terrorist enemy that is still revered by millions of poor excluded people who identify with Islam. Although both the authors reveal a deep respect for the Muslim religion and its practices, they are more frightened of the creeping fundamentalism in the restrictions on what the faithful may read or wear than on the terrorists and their bombs. The danger is that the Islamic bombers in their despair and the American bombing response to them will drive ordinary Arab Muslims into outbreaks of uncontrollable violence against their own people as well as against the infidel. In the last resort the West has to do something to correct, and to correct soon, what bin Ladin knows are the hurts that arouse most anger among Arab Muslims – the discrimination suffered everywhere by Muslim immigrants, the failure to stop the Israelis occupying the whole of Palestine, the continuing support for the dictatorship of the Saudi family over Saudi Arabia, and the pitiless sanctions against the people of Iraq.

If something is not done to make a start towards these corrections, bombing in Afghanistan and the introduction of Western troops into that unhappy country, whether they capture bin Laden and defeat the Taliban armies or not, will lead to endless war in Central Asia. We have seen in Israel, in Chechnya, in Dagestan, in Kosovo, in the Philippines and now in New York what anger and frustration drives people to do. The question of the future control over Caspian oil supplies and the balance of power in Eurasia cannot be solved by force of arms. Only a genuine attempt to feed and care for starving people, to find homes for refugees and asylum seekers and to reach long term solutions within the United Nations rubric to the use of the planet's resources and their fair distribution will possibly prevent a vicious cycle of accumulating violence. For what does war than still more war portend?

Michael Barratt Brown

Indonesian turmoil

Roland Challis, *Shadow of a Revolution: Indonesia and the Generals*, Sutton Publishing, 260 pp, £19.99, ISBN 0750924535

Roland Challis was South East Asia correspondent of the BBC during the tumultuous years of the Indonesian turmoil of the 1960s. This story was known on the left for many years, and has been told before. But the fact that Challis had a ringside seat, and that he was able to stay the course, means that this is a very useful book. It is all the more useful for being a truthful account.

It explains how Britain and the United States conspired to undermine, and then replace President Sukarno, the initial founder of Indonesia and leader of its struggle for independence from Dutch colonists. Sukarno was a genuine nationalist, whose commitment was to maintain freedom from both Communism and Western capitalism. He clashed with the British over the creation of the Malaysian Federation, and the CIA began a systematic infiltration of the Indonesian army, by suborning likely Generals. The Americans applied the same techniques over and again, most recently in respect of West European Social Democrats, who were suborned by the Committee for the Successor Generation.

In Indonesia there were fewer restraints, and when the moment came, the CIA and British counter-insurgents furnished their favoured generals with lists of more than a million alleged Communists, most of whom were thereupon slaughtered. The rivers ran red with the blood of Indonesian peasants and their teachers, and General Suharto, who had been talent-spotted by the Americans, became the new Indonesian President.

This massacre was the worst in post-war history, but it was almost completely concealed from the people of the Western world. Thousands of political prisoners were also detained in concentration camps, and many of them were kept there until as recently as 1998.

Roland Challis has been able to augment his own personal experience by access to archive material which has only recently been released. The Suharto regime became a byword for corruption and repressive cruelty, and Indonesia a basket case for the violation of human rights. Suharto ruled for three decades, during which internal tensions wracked Indonesia as the Government was ever more openly identified with various forms of depravity.

Challis does not shrink from documenting the fall of Suharto, and the continuing pressures of the United States Government on his successors. This is an important book, which will contribute to an awakening of concern about the methods of the American Empire, of which it provides a paradigm case. The destruction of Indonesian Communism was also the destruction of any possibility of secular reform, so that corruption is not outfaced by religious fundamentalism.

Will Indonesia chart the development of a wider doom?

M. K. Weil

War and Want

Gwyn Kirk and Margo Okazawa-Rey (editors), *Neoliberalism, Militarism and Armed Conflict (Social Justice* journal, vol.27, no.4), 2000, 172 pp, $12.95, from Social Justice, PO Box 40601, San Francisco, CA 94140, USA, ISSN 0094-7571

'The globalisation of the world economy will continue, with a widening between 'haves' and 'have-nots'...'

United States Space Command Vision for 2020

The stark mission statement of the United States Space Command reads 'US

Space Command dominating the space dimension of military operations to protect US national interests and investment'. That is their proposed solution to the perceived threat from the millions of people across great regions of the world who have little or nothing. Those millions might strike back in some way at the destruction of their livelihoods demanded by the World Trade Organisation and other remote institutions in the name of 'open markets'.

The World Trade Organisation (WTO) is a prime instrument in the drive to globalise economic activity in the interests of large corporations. In so doing, it fosters inequalities and other conditions that can cause unrest, conflict and even war. At the same time, it systematically undermines public provision and service in many sectors. Governments are discouraged from directly providing health, education and other basic services. According to the WTO, they should increasingly contract out these functions to private corporations.

But, while it attacks governments' social and environmental policies, which may reduce corporate profits, the World Trade Organisation accords an altogether different status to government spending on military matters. As Steven Staples emphasises in this very rich collection, Article XXI of the General Agreement on Tariffs and Trade (GATT) affords governments a free reign for actions taken in the interest of national security. Thus, the World Trade Organisation actually protects actions by governments to develop, arm, and deploy armed forces and supply their military establishments. This translates into protection of the profits of the major corporations engaged in the arms trade.

An example illustrates the point. In 1999, a WTO trade panel ruled against a programme of the Canadian Government which subsidised the production of civilian aircraft by aerospace and defence corporations. The Canadian authorities quickly announced a new $30 million subsidy programme for the same Canadian corporations, but this time the money went towards the production of new weapons (*Canadian Press* 18 October 1999).

Contrast this with the billions of dollars which the Pentagon pays to American weapons corporations. They receive a substantial part of the now over $400-billion US military budget. In turn, a significant proportion of these payments are, in effect, corporate subsidies. But, because the corporations are making weapons, the subsidy is protected under GATT's Article XXI.

In recent years, the weapons merchants in North America and Europe have merged their companies at a rapid rate. Until the late 1990s, transatlantic mergers of defence/military contractors had been prohibited by national governments on the grounds of national security concerns. Then, in 1999, the Pentagon signalled the inevitable merger of US and European military corporations when it awarded BAe Systems (formerly British Aerospace) military contracts as if it was an American corporation.

Now, a handful of giant corporations dominate this lucrative business in the United States. For the year 2000, the five biggest US arms corporations (Lockheed Martin, Boeing, Raytheon, Northrop Grumman, TRW) received prime contracts from the Pentagon worth $41.3 billion (see Bob Aldridge, 'The

Weapons Merchants', *The Spokesman*, no.72, p.54). In the United States, they exercise great influence on government policy, particularly in the area of military procurement. At the same time, they are able to dominate the lucrative global arms trade, with many customers in Third World countries.

Thus, in the words of Bob Aldridge, 'for may years the overriding impetus behind the arms race, and now the ballistic missile race, has been the profits earned from weapons manufacture and the other types of exploitation that superpower status protects.'

As globalisation extends the reach of corporate interests around the world, a matching military capacity is deployed to protect those interests. Now, as the epigraph shows, the US military looks to the heavens to fulfil this task. But the peace, environmental, and anti-globalisation movements have an alternative vision for the years ahead. After the desperate slaughter of September 11, armaments budgets are increasing when they should be cut. At the same time, regulation of arms sales is being reduced when it should be increased. But, as we have seen, arms spending is protected by World Trade Organisation rules. This unacceptable situation is now a pressing priority for the global anti-capitalist movement.

This thought underpins much of the analysis of the connections which make up the corporate-military state, which forms the first part of this extensive collection. It ranges from Sierra Leone to Palestine and Yugoslavia, and from diamonds and water disputes to state crime and civil society. Part two considers 'visions of global security and sustainability', with an emphasis on the work of women's organisations. Again, the range is wide, from the Children's Movement for Peace in Colombia to the declaration of the African Women's Anti-War Coalition to Women's Pentagon Action.

Above all, we need to join together to create and safeguard a democratic space in which people can develop rational responses, and look for peaceful alternatives to the burgeoning militarisation of world affairs. This volume helps in that work.

Tony Simpson

Public Transport

Andrew Murray, *Off the Rails: Britain's Great Rail Crisis - Cause, Consequences and Cure*, Verso, 198 pp. £14 hardback ISBN 1859846408

Andrew Murray works for ASLEF, the train drivers' union. He therefore has access to an unparalleled range of public and private sources of information about the staggering crisis of Britain's rail system. This book chronicles the paralysis of the network after the Hatfield disaster, but it also explains the underlying structures which have wrecked the privatised railways.

Andrew Murray has mounted a comprehensive indictment of privatisation, especially in the areas of safety. He offers convincing analysis of the accidents at Southall, Ladbroke Grove and Hatfield, and shows that in spite of their different causes, all are traceable to the shortcomings of privatisation.

This book provides a platform from which railway workers themselves can speak. The stress under which they have been compelled to work is poignantly highlighted in these pages.

'The evidence is' he writes, 'that politicians who grasp the mettle of re-nationalising the railway will lose nothing in terms of public esteem or votes. Banishing the one hundred piece railway to the past will earn some political leader a place in the history books.'

A worthy hope this. But where shall we find such a leader? Hardly will he or she emerge from the present British Parliament, or from the political parties which are present in it. *Off the Rails* is an indictment, not only of the privatised railway system, but of British political institutions, which are entirely uninterested in the public good.

JB

Where are the Foot Soldiers?

Greg Rosen (Ed), *Dictionary of Labour Biography,* Politico's with the Fabian Society. 664pp. £30 ISBN 1902301188

James Callaghan provided the foreword to this heavy Dictionary, saying that

> 'It brings to life the politics of the Labour Party, past and present, through the personalities who shaped it. It recalls the courage and conviction of those who fought to build and renew the Party they loved over the past century, and the trauma of the fraternal battles that weakened it.'

Many of the protagonists are indeed featured in this biographical *tour de force*, although it is hardly strengthened by the view that its fraternal battles weakened the Party. All mass movements evolve, and enjoy their times of dynamism and growth, after which they are prone to slide into inertia, or even decline. The fortunate movements are those which go on to enjoy renewal. And where would that come from, were it not for the readiness to embark upon 'fraternal battles'?

The trouble is, that many of the vital arguments in the Labour Party have been initiated by relatively unknown people, and most of the dedicated protagonists have not found their way into the House of Commons. But almost all of the cast list of this big volume have been in Parliament, while many of them have also found their way into the House of Lords. To provide a picture of the Labour Movement at its best, the focus would need to shift in order to depict far more of the work of the foot soldiers, as well as the barrack room lawyers who have enlivened this army.

Among the many interesting portraits featured is Matt Carter's sketch of the life of R. H. Tawney, who refused the offer of a peerage by Ramsay MacDonald in 1933, 'replying "What harm have I ever done to the Labour Party?"' But Matt Carter thinks that Tawney's ideas have subsequently influenced successive Labour leaders from Gaitskell through to Blair. There is very little evidence of this: Blair's Christianity was extracted from the same polluted well as his socialism, so that Tawney might very well ask us what harm had he ever done us, that we should seek to pin responsibility for New Labour on his broad shoulders.

June Castle

Left Book Club

Paul Laity (ed.) *Left Book Club Anthology*, pp. 254, Victor Gollancz, 2001, Hb. £20 (discount through *New Statesman* Book Club) ISBN 0575072210

It was an idea that Gollancz would have approved of to republish excerpts from some of the most famous of the Left Book Club titles from the late 1930s, just as political discourse is beginning to recover from the blanketing of New Labour. In 1936, Gollancz, urged on by Stafford Cripps, John Strachey and Harold Laski, saw this publishing enterprise not just as a money spinner but, in his words, as a 'matter of terrible urgency at the present time, when the world is drifting into war, and fascism is triumphing in country after country.' Sixty five years later we face a situation that is not so dissimilar, and could do with something of the huge enthusiasm generated by the publications and associated activities organised by the Club. By 1939, there were 57,000 members with 1200 local discussion groups, through which the two hundred and more titles were sold at 2s6d each (an eighth of a £ then – £4 roughly today). Total sales amounted to millions of copies. Why not today?

There is one major difference. There appeared then to be an alternative to capitalism. The Left still saw the Soviet Union as the bastion of resistance to fascism and as 'a new civilisation?', the subtitle of Sidney and Beatrice Webb's study of the Soviet Union, published in a Left Book Club edition without the question mark. What doubts there were about the Communist leadership in the Club's organisation were repressed, and about Soviet socialism actually suppressed. Gollancz, like Strachey and Laski a Communist Party 'fellow traveller', as they were then called, refused to publish the Trotskyist C.L.R. James, but published Leon Feuchtwanger's *Moscow 1937*, and J.R.Campbell's *Soviet Policy and Its Critics*, both written in defence of the Moscow Trials . He refused to publish Orwell's Homage to Catalonia because it revealed Spanish Communists under Russian trained commissars fighting against their Anarchist allies. Gollancz only published Orwell's best selling *Road to Wigan Pier* (42,000 copies) with a foreword by himself, dissociating the Club from Orwell's excoriating criticism of middle class socialists (Orwell went to Eton!), feminists, pacifists, vegetarians and other cranks who Orwell believed besmirched the cause of socialism.

Another major difference lies in the condition of the people – at least in Britain and other industrialised countries. Things may not be good for many people in Britain today, faced by unemployment and poverty. A third of our children are in families living below the poverty line. But that is a relative figure, measured in relation to average incomes, and the average has undoubtedly risen since the 1930s. The housing conditions described by Orwell, the working conditions described by Bert Coombes in *These Poor Hands*, or the lot of the unemployed as seen by Wal Hannington in his *Ten Lean Years* would not be found today except in the Third World, and there only too often. Inequality is as great today as in the 1930s, ostentatious wealth even more obscene than then, but protest is dulled by the general aura of affluence in countries like Britain.

A third difference is that, however frightening the prospect of American 'full spectrum dominance', star wars to come and land wars now in the Middle East and Afghanistan, the United States does not look like the dictatorships of Hitler, Mussolini or the other fascist regimes of the 1930s; and of course in many respects it is not like them. There are no marching brown shirts and black shirts. Considerable freedoms exist and some democratic controls over government; and racism is not overt. The talons, moreover, of the American eagle are not felt in Europe but in far away places. And yet it seemed like that in the late 1920s and early 30s before economic recession had gone far and the dictators had seized power. It was then that a Left Book Club found its time had come. Perhaps, 70 years later the time has come again.

Those of us who grew up in the 1930s and learnt our first Marxist economics from John Strachey's *Theory and Practice of Socialism*, a 1936 Left Book Club choice, accepted Communist leadership and Soviet practice without much question. Capitalism had brought the slump and fascism with it. Communists were fighting fascism in Spain and building a popular front with the Socialists in France. We thought that we were in good company in the Club. Authors included Arthur Koestler (*Spanish Testament*), Edgar Snow (*Red Star over China*), Clement Attlee (*Labour Party in Perspective*), Stephen Spender (*Forward from Liberalism*), J.B.S. Haldane (*Air-Raid Precautions*), A.L. Morton (*Peoples' History of England*), Leonard Woolf (*Barbarians at the Gate*), Clifford Odets (*Waiting for Lefty*).

The excerpts in this volume include Gollancz's preface and two chapters of *Wigan Pier*, chapters from Arthur Koestler, from Edgar Snow, from Stephen Spender and most of the introduction to Strachey's *Theory and Practice*. In addition there are splendid passages on prison life from Wilfred Macartney's *Walls have Mouths*, on Berlin under the Nazis from Jan Petersen's *Our Street*, on life in Austria under the Nazis by G.E.R. Gedye (*Fallen Bastions*), on the life of a coal miner by Bert Coombes (*These Poor Hands*). The cultural outreach of the Club's activities is illustrated not only by the excerpt from Odets' play *Waiting for Lefty*, but by inclusion of some poems by Randall Swingler and the introduction from Alan Bush and Randall Swingler's *Left Song Book*, used in so many left-wing group gatherings thereafter.

As I look along the long shelves of fading orange covered books, there are several that this anthology has missed out, which I should have included excerpts from: Ellen Wilkinson's story of Jarrow, *The Town that was Murdered*, André Malraux's novel, *Days of Contempt*, Konni Zilliacus's history of the League of Nations in *Mirror of the Past*, G.D.H. Cole's concept of *The People's Front* and his lessons for *Britain in the Post-war World*, Leonard Barnes's *Empire or Democracy*, Simon Haxey's profiles in his *Tory MP*, but these are matters of personal interest. The question raised for us today is how books like the New Statesman Book Club selections or the Spokesman Socialist Renewal series and meetings of the Socialist Alliance groups could begin to attract the sort of numbers that the Left Book Club attracted.

What effect did it all have? Orwell believed that if the war against Germany and Italy and later Japan did not become a revolutionary war, it would end up with a sell-out to the dictators. It didn't; perhaps in part because the middle classes, influenced by the Left Book Club, were not so wet after all as Orwell supposed but saw the war as a war against fascism. And it is wrong to suppose that Club members were all middle class. In Sheffield, for example, the local organiser was Bill Owen who became district officer of the Transport and General Workers' Union and secretary of the Sheffield Trades Council. The Communist Party had strong links with the unions and the unemployed workers' organisations and a tradition of educational classes. Nye Bevan believed that the Club 'prepared the way' for Labour's victory in 1945. I think that that was only true via the radicalisation of the conscript army, and in that process the Army Bureau of Current Affairs, often staffed by Left Book Club members, played its part. We should never despair of the effect of the written word. In these days of endless government spin, we need serious books more than ever before.

Michael Barratt Brown

Kenneth Tynan

John Lahr (Ed), *The Diaries of Kenneth Tynan*, Bloomsbury 440 pp. £25 ISBN 0747554188

Kenneth Tynan was a critic who wielded great influence, and aroused strong affections. I can speak personally, because, as a young coal miner, I discovered his column in *The Observer* and came to follow it keenly, with avidity. From Tynan I learned about Brecht, although I could not, in those days, ever see Brecht performed in our provincial theatres. Instead, I had to read Eric Bentley's translations in our public library. They were expensively imported from the United States. But then, in one of the most momentous experiences in my life, Tynan broke the news, and incited all of us to take the train to London in order to see *Mother Courage*, performed by the Berliner Ensemble on the London stage. I found it a truly unforgettable experience, even though I spoke no

German. Of course, I knew about the play, but I was totally unprepared for the extraordinary staging: the design, and the colours, above all those colours.

Several times in those days I made that journey down to London, always in response to the same incitement, to see John Osborne's *Look Back in Anger*, and then to be spell-bound by *Waiting for Godot*.

The West End theatre was not a comfortable place for a gauche and puritanical proletarian, and I can remember the culture shock at another performance of the *Threepenny Opera*, when I found myself surrounded by people I saw as unbelievable toffs. Now I would suspect them to have been a normal part of London's theatre-going public.

The Sunday papers were already famous in the 1950s for their nodding acquaintance with serious matters. The literary fashion was to glance in towards knowledge: to pretend to understand by hints and catchphrases, so that it could be presumed that what had to be known was shared by all. But nodding at knowledge usually concealed an ignorance made invincible by condescension. How many reviewers made their living by practising this trade! But Tynan was not like that. His criticism was written for people who wanted to know. He took his readers earnestly seriously. His intellectual honesty was instantly appealing to those who wanted to know.

It is, for this reason, a bit sad that most people remember Kenneth Tynan as the first person to say fuck on television. Of course, this was a political statement: and it was intended as a blow against national hypocrisy.

National hypocrisy survives, and indeed thrives, although the extent to which it has taken on board uncouth expressions and louche behaviour is perhaps marked out in these diaries, which probably no longer shock, even if, at the time, they would have been deemed sensational. John Lahr has given us a picture of the private Tynan, which of course includes the critic, and some part of the commitment. It also includes a prolonged sado-masochistic affair, and all sorts of other stunts which might today have won coverage for a day in the tabloid press. As often happens, the pursuit of pleasure seems to have made Tynan miserable: a fact which makes itself apparent behind all the naughty confessions and humorous goings-on.

The cast of this book is enormous, and includes a most remarkable cross-section of the glitterati. Princess Margaret roisters with the Tynans, and takes in a blue movie. Various less eminent ladies are extensively spanked and give rise to frank reports about their enjoyment of the experience. Dislikes are paraded freely, and there are at least a couple of remarkable feuds, with other directors, and with Harold Pinter.

All of this sizzling material will ensure that John Lahr's presentation will be widely read, and perhaps even enjoyed. I don't know how this will affect people who were close to Tynan, either as family or friends. It doesn't raise my spirits, because I prefer the Tynan I never met, but who I followed into the theatre during one of the most exciting intellectual experiences of my life.

Ken Coates

Poker

David Edmonds and John Eidinow, *Wittgenstein's Poker*, Faber and Faber 2001, 267 pp. hardback £9.99, ISBN057120547X

Two impassioned people with troubled but different histories met in a small room in King's College, Cambridge, in 1946. The setting was predominantly male-oriented academia in the exhausted aftermath of World War Two. They may, or may not, have come to blows. They were both Viennese Jews with experience of the anschluss, but they brought with them two very different philosophical bents.

On the one hand, Wittgenstein believed that we could be extricated from philosophical problems by freeing ourselves from language based confusions. In other words, we have to stop ourselves from becoming bewitched by our use of language.

On the other hand, Popper believed that many philosophical arguments, such as those bearing on politics and scientific discovery, are dealing with problems that go beyond language itself. This belief he shared with Russell, also present at the meeting, who spent a good deal of his life addressing controversies in politics and science.

Wittgenstein's Poker brings together the different versions of what happened during this single confrontation between two philosophers who have left behind very different intellectual legacies. This book also emphasises the fact that confused memories of the incident do not detract from the importance of the content of the fight. It was a fight over what philosophy should be about, and this debate still continues over fifty years later.

Wittgenstein's Poker is an enjoyable and funny book which investigates 20th Century philosophy and the antipathies within it. How much the personal biographies of the two philosophers shaped their approach to the debate is an issue raised clearly here, without obscuring the importance of this zealous search for the right answers to big questions.

Pamela White

C. Wright Mills

Kathryn and Pamela Mills (editors), C. Wright Mills: *Letters and Autobiographical Writings,* University of California Press, 378 pp £21.95 cloth ISBN 0520211065

In a labour of love, the daughters of C. Wright Mills have selected 150 of his surviving letters, some autobiographical essays from one of his manuscripts, and a number of other significant writings. They have sought to offer a picture of their father's wide commitments, and to reflect not only his powerful contribution to the social sciences, but also his other interests from motor cycles to international politics.

Some of us were already familiar with Wright Mills' correspondence, because he expressed himself by means of open letters, such as that which he sent to the New Left, or those about Cuba which he wrote for his book *Listen, Yankee* in an attempt to awaken America to the significance of what was happening in Cuba. The Mills daughters contribute haunting essays in memory of their father, and many of us share in their sense of loss.

Mills' English correspondents included Edward Thompson and Ralph Miliband. His American correspondence features exchanges with Saul Alinsky, Daniel Bell, Carlos Fuentes, Irving Howe, Dwight MacDonald, Robert K. Merton and David Riesman.

C. Wright Mills still repays close study. His books, *White Collar* and *The Power Elite*, still belong in every Socialist library. This touching memoir serves to bring their author closer to us.

M. Osbourne

Star Wars

Karl Grossman, *Weapons in Space,* Seven Stories Press, New York, 88pp, £4.99, ISBN 1583220445

Karl Grossman has been a tireless campaigner against the militarisation of space, upon which hundreds of billions of dollars are to be spent over the next few years. In this pamphlet, he exposes the military preparations of the United States, and documents the activities of the US Space Command, a summary of whose plans was recently published in *The Spokesman* pamphlet, *Straw Wars - Full Spectrum Sycophancy*.

The plan to fill up space with high-powered military lasers and other sci-fi devices seems not to have been impeded by the attack on the Twin Towers in New York, even though this was accomplished by a small group of suicide attackers armed with Stanley knives, who could not be intercepted from space, or even anticipated from space-based eavesdroppers.

Grossman summarises the thinking of a whole series of menacing 'defence experts' such as George and Meredith Friedman, authors of *The Future of War: Power, Technology and American World Dominance in the 21st Century*. 'The age of the gun is over' they say. 'He who controls space controls the battlefield.' But not, apparently, the territory of the World Trade Centre.

Bin Laden has reduced the doctrine of Full Spectrum Dominance to absurdity, but this does not mean that it has been aborted. Instead, we now face two dire threats, each equally absurd, and both devoid of any humanitarian principle.

Karl Grossman's pamphlet should be very widely read, because it will open minds to one of the major sources of wickedness in the world.

JP